Everyday Harumi

SIMPLE JAPANESE FOOD FOR FAMILY & FRIENDS

Photography by Jason Lowe

conran OCTOPUS

Contents

Introduction

I have said many times that I consider myself to be an ordinary housewife, and in so many ways that is what I still am. I still prepare meals for my husband, family, and friends and I still look after the house and the housework. But there are not many housewives who have had the opportunities to travel as extensively and meet so many people as I have and I am truly thankful for those chances.

I have been able to look at Japan from the outside, to see my compatriots and, most importantly for me, look at Japanese food and its character. I believe that it is impossible to truly know your own country without looking at it from the outside and seeing how it is viewed by others. This applies to my journey with Japanese cuisine.

My first two books, *Harumi's Japanese Cooking* and *Harumi's Japanese Home Cooking* were created from recipes that I made for my readers in Japan. This book, *Everyday Harumi*, has been created in a completely different way and in one that reflects my own personal journey. So what has happened? I think that I have, through my travels, friendships, and work, come to understand how different cultures work like different languages. There are things that can be translated directly while some concepts need to be explained more fully. What is at the heart of Japanese food are the building blocks, the tools we work with, and I am hoping that with this book you will discover what Japanese cuisine is and how to cook it for yourself.

I believe that eating healthily is an essential principle in Japanese food. It is lighter than other cuisines, it is low in fat, and is particularly low in dairy. It is not a vegetarian cuisine but it recognizes the crucial importance of vegetables in the overall balance of a meal. It also places importance on eating vegetables seasonally and I get great pleasure from taking the time to select vegetables that are at their best. I really love the addition of at least one or two vegetable dishes to a meal, especially if the vegetables are still nice and crunchy, and you will find in this book a wide array of delicious recipes for vegetables.

Japanese portions also tend to be smaller, helping to keep people slim. If you want to lose weight I recommend you look to adopting a Japanese diet and eat less in volume but more in terms of good things like vegetables—two of the central principles of Japanese food.

Many of the recipes contained in this book are the staples of home cooking in Japan. They reflect the average family's repetoire. These recipes are very simple because I hope that they will help introduce you to typical Japanese sauces and dressings and ways of cooking that might be very new but are not difficult.

There is a different way of both cooking and eating in Japan to that in Western cultures. I think it can be said that Japanese food is primarily about variety; variety of flavors and textures and this should drive your selection of recipes. I would never prepare a meal of just deep-fried dishes, equally we would not serve only tofu recipes.

It is also about certain flavors and ingredients. Many recipes are based on a mixture of soy sauce, mirin, dashi, and sake and without these ingredients it would be hard to create a real Japanese flavor. I made this book in Britain and, as I was creating the recipes, I was checking what was available, trying to find simple ways of bringing Japanese food to the table. But as I was cooking I was also learning about the differences in ingredients and discovering new flavors.

Presentation is another essential element in Japanese food. Food should be presented with thought and care. I love spending time choosing the right plates or bowls to serve food on—I want the

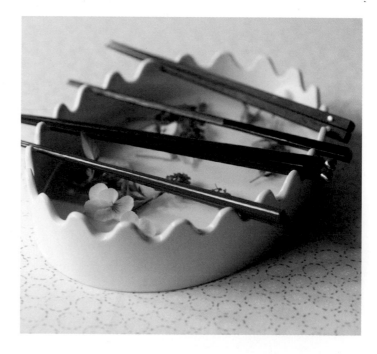

designs of the dishes to complement and work with my cooking. The serving dishes you choose don't necessarily have to be expensive but they do have to suit the food as well as match the occasion.

Equally, I enjoy thinking about what type of drink to serve with my food and I will offer ice-cold Japanese beer, hot or cold sake, shochu or wine, depending on the flavors of the food and the season.

Presentation is not just a matter of choosing the dishes to serve your food on, it is also important how the food itself looks. I am always very concerned about how ingredients are prepared and am usually quite specific about the size into which ingredients should be cut. Obviously, part of this is due to the fact that in Japan we traditionally eat with chopsticks and so need to have food in easy to eat portions, but I think it also affects the taste of the ingredient. I suggest you try cutting fresh ginger in different ways if you want to understand what I mean—minced, finely julienned, sliced, or simply peeled—each way creates a different taste.

In Japanese there are many words for the different styles of cutting and I must admit I often find it frustrating trying to find the equivalent words in English. In fact, if you go to any bookshop in Japan and look in the recipe book section you will find that any cookbook for beginners contains sections on the different ways in which vegetables, meat, and fish can be cut. I think this is one of those areas where it is hard to translate, but if you want to replicate Japanese food it is a good element to work at.

Like most people who enjoy cooking, I love wandering around local markets and supermarkets. Even though I was in London to work on this book, I greatly enjoyed looking around the many food stores and seeing what was available. It all looked so different from my supermarket in Japan. The opportunity to experiment with new ingredients and create new recipes has been very inspiring for me.

So what is different between Japanese and Western ingredients? I think that one of the obvious differences is the size of the vegetables. For example, eggplants are very small in Japan, as are cucumbers. Other differences are less obvious; carrots and ginger are softer and easier to chop and grate in Japan and we have more types of mushrooms. Leeks are one of the biggest differences. In Japan we have a whole range of different leeks and once their names are translated it does not always give you the exact same ingredient.

As for meat, here again the selection is quite different. We value some fat on or in meat. It adds flavor and makes it tender when cooked. I can find chicken thighs without bones but with skin in any supermarket. I can also easily find ground chicken at home—but in London I had to go to a butchers and ask specifically for it to be made.

Fish was a real surprise. I found the most delicious fish in London and would recommend the mackerel to anyone. However, it was hard to find the same range of fish as we have in Japan, especially the range of sashimi (raw fish).

I also came to realize that not only were the ingredients different but people's choices were different, too. I have asked many non-Japanese, "What do you always have in your refrigerator?" and have been surprised by the replies. I usually have daikon, tofu, and natto. In London it seemed that broccoli and celery were most common.

So how can we bridge the gap between Japan and the rest of the world in terms of cooking? Some would say that without all the ingredients being Japanese it is impossible to make authentic Japanese food. I have even heard that some Japanese chefs working outside of Japan will have water imported from Japan in order to create absolutely "authentic" Japanese food. I think this is extreme and would not for one moment suggest that you need to do that to make a Japanese meal at home. Certainly, even within the geographical borders of Japan there are many differences in the natural ingredients of each area as there are differences in these ingredients, depending on the season.

Good quality ingredients, wherever they come from, should be celebrated, eaten seasonally whenever possible, and treated with respect when prepared. Nearly all can be used in Japanese food. The trick is to select the right sauce, dressing, or preparation for the specific ingredient. In this book, I have tried to present a wide variety of very basic, typically Japanese recipes and I think you will be able to create fantastic meals using these simple flavors and easy methods. There are, however, some specific ingredients and sauces that I consider to be essential to cook a Japanese meal, which I have listed on the following pages. I think it is worth buying these items and keeping them in your cupboard or refrigerator so you can, when the mood takes you, create a Japanese meal with whatever other ingredients you happen to have. In fact, I think that Japanese housewives who are still the main cooks at home, though it is changing, are probably the most competent cooks in the world with kitchen cupboards full of international ingredients. We can cook Japanese one night, followed by Chinese, by Italian, or Thai. We love trying food from around the world and have the building blocks to be able to create many types of cuisine. I think I am lucky to live in a culture that really loves food—all types as long as it is good!

I would like to see people around the world doing the same with Japanese food, being able to say "I feel like eating Japanese food tonight. What shall I make?' and then making it easily.

The recipes in this book are all dishes I like to cook everyday at home. So as long as you have the staple kitchen cupboard ingredients (see page 17) they should all be quick and easy to make and I hope you enjoy making them as much as I do.

Kitchen cupboard essentials

So what do you need to get started? I think these are all absolute essentials for your kitchen cupboard:

Japanese sushi rice
Japanese soy sauce
mirin
katsuobushi (dried fish flakes)/and or instant dashi stock
toasted sesame seeds
miso
sake
rice vinegar
noodles like soba and udon
tofu
potato starch (katakuriko)
kombu seaweed (dried kelp)
nori seaweed
wasabi
fresh ginger and garlic
superfine sugar

With these essentials, you can create most of the sauces and dressings in this book and make a large variety of easy everyday Japanese meals. The sauces and dressings on the following pages are very much the cornerstones of many dishes and can be made in advance and stored in the fridge, thereby making it easier to just create a recipe.

Japanese rice
Rice is a central ingredient in Japanese cuisine. For us it is one of the most important elements of a meal. I love the simplicity and taste of a bowl of Japanese white rice—it is something I always long for after a trip overseas.

If you get to know the taste of Japanese rice you will soon realize that the flavor changes according to where it is grown, when it is harvested, and what variety it is. So when I am planning a dish I am always thinking about which rice to use. Unfortunately, there are not so many varieties of Japanese rice available outside Japan but if you have the opportunity to try a new one, please do so.

Japanese rice is very special. It is in many ways a symbol of Japan and is at the heart of most Japanese meals. Unlike the long-grain rice or basmati rice commonly used outside Japan, this rice is short grain and very sticky, which makes it much easier to eat with chopsticks.

Although you could use long-grain rice in some of these recipes, it would not be authentically Japanese, so I would strongly recommend that you find a supply of good Japanese rice. I would also recommend you learn how to cook it properly.

Cooking rice

When I cook rice I pay close attention to the details of its preparation. I always wash it thoroughly in cold water, measure the correct amount of water to cook it in, and time the cooking as well as the time it needs to sit before serving. Preparation is very important.

Like most Japanese, I use a rice cooker at home but, because not everyone has one at home overseas, I would like to introduce you to a method of cooking rice using a saucepan.

SERVES 4

11 oz Japanese white sushi rice

1. Wash the rice before cooking it—you need to put the rice in a bowl, add some water, then gently rub the grains together. Tip the water away. At first you will see the water is very cloudy but as you repeat this action you will soon find the water becomes clear.
2. When the water is clear, drain the rice. It can be used immediately if necessary, but for the best result it should be left in a strainer for 10–15 minutes.
3. Put the rice in a heavy saucepan and add 1⅔ cups water. You should generally add the same amount of water as rice but if you want the rice to be softer, then add a little more water. Cover with a lid and bring to a boil.
4. When it is boiling, turn the heat down and simmer for 10–12 minutes, then turn off the heat and leave it to stand for a further 10 minutes. During the whole process you should not remove the lid.
5. Gently fold the rice inward, away from the sides of the saucepan and then put in either one large serving dish or in separate bowls.

Katsuobushi (dried fish flakes)

Katsuobushi are the shavings from a dried bonito fish. These shavings are the foundation of one of the most important elements of Japanese flavoring—dashi. They are also used to garnish and add flavor to a variety of recipes. In Japan they are sold in different-sized packages. It is worth buying a few packages and keeping them in your cupboard because they last well.

Dashi stock

One of the most important ingredients in a Japanese dish is good dashi stock. Although you can buy instant dashi everywhere I always make my own and there is always some ready to use in my refrigerator. I like to have quite a strongly flavored dashi and so add quite a lot of the katsuobushi, the dried fish flakes that give dashi its unique flavor. Many people who make their own dashi stock will make what is known as ichiban dashi (the first brew) and niban dashi (the second brew). The first is usually used when you need a pure dashi flavor and the second when it is mixed with other ingredients. I believe this habit comes from days when the katsuobushi was rare and expensive, so could not be wasted. In my recipes I always use "ichiban dashi," unless otherwise indicated.

Ichiban dashi stock

8 × 4 inch pieces kombu seaweed (dried kelp)
2 oz katsuobushi (dried fish flakes)

1. Put 4 cups water in a large saucepan. To remove any excess saltiness from the kombu, either quickly wash it under cold running water and then pat dry or wipe with a damp cloth. Add to the cooking water, leaving it to soak for 30 minutes.
2. Put the saucepan over high heat and remove the kombu just before the water comes to a boil. Add the katsuobushi, bring back to a boil, and then immediately turn off the heat.
3. Let it stand until all the flakes have sunk to the bottom of the saucepan.
4. Pour the mixture through a strainer lined with paper towel, leave to cool, and keep the dashi stock in the refrigerator until ready to use. Do not discard the used katsuobushi if you want to make a niban dashi stock.

Niban dashi stock

1. Add the previously used kombu seaweed and katsuobushi to a saucepan together with 4 cups water. Put the pan onto medium heat.
2. Remove the kombu seaweed just before the liquid comes to a boil, then cook for a further 3–4 minutes.
3. Pour through a strainer lined with paper towel and again, cool, and store in the refrigerator until ready to use.

You can keep premade dashi stock in the fridge for a couple of days or in the freezer for up to 1 week.

Sake

It is possible to buy sake almost anywhere in the world now. This internationally known rice wine is a very useful addition to sauces and marinades. Although there may be a wide range on offer, I would suggest that for cooking purposes, almost any make will suffice. It is also a good drink to serve with all Japanese meals, either hot or cold.

Japanese soy sauce

I don't want to seem too biased here but I do think that Japanese soy sauce works better in Japanese recipes than the soy sauce from other countries. I think it is worth looking for. Buy a large bottle— at least a 17fl oz size—it is more economical and will save you having to go to the grocery store half way through a recipe! You will also notice that I sometimes call for light soy sauce in my recipes. I use this as an alternative to regular soy sauce in recipes where a lighter-colored soy sauce is preferable, but if you cannot find light soy sauce, just use regular soy sauce.

Mirin

You will find mirin in many of my recipes—it is ubiquitous in Japanese cooking. Mirin is a sweet transparent liquid with a low alcohol content. It keeps well even when opened. I have looked at finding substitutes for mirin but it is not easy to find an alternative ingredient that performs as mirin does —it adds a sweetness and a silkiness to sauces and dressings that is quite unique.

Toasted sesame seeds

Every Japanese supermarket sells a variety of packages of toasted sesame seeds and sesame seed products. You can buy black or white sesame seeds, whole seeds or ground seeds, sesame sauce, sesame salad dressing, sesame paste—the list is endless. I think it is a really typical flavor in Japanese cooking and it is one I personally love.

My mother makes all her sesame pastes herself and will happily spend the time needed to grind the seeds by hand in her large Japanese suribachi mortar. These mortars are very clever and very beautiful; they are grooved on the inside so facilitating the grinding of the seeds. Traditionally, long wooden pestles, made from the wood of the Japanese prickly ash (sansho) tree, are used with these mortars.

Sesame seeds last well, so it is worth having them in your cupboard. However, make sure that you use them up fairly soon after purchasing because, over time, they lose their lovely aroma. Once a package has been opened you should store it in an airtight container. If possible try to find sesame seeds that are already toasted. In Japan we have a wonderful gadget for toasting seeds but because it is hard to find internationally you will probably have to heat them carefully over a low heat in a small skillet—they do smell heavenly. Please do not use untoasted seeds for any of these recipes.

Miso

Made from fermented soy beans, miso is a wonderful ingredient that can be used in sauces, soups, or marinades. It is the basis for the most famous Japanese soup, miso shiru. Again, there are many different types of miso, each with their own particular flavor and characteristics. I have used something called "awase miso" in most of these recipes which is a mix of red and white miso pastes and is fairly standard in its taste, but if you can't easily find this then just use a miso that you can find in your local store that is neither too sweet nor too salty. Sold in tubs, miso should be kept stored in a refrigerator.

Rice vinegar

In my house I have many different types of vinegars, such as balsamic vinegar or wine vinegar, but for most traditional Japanese recipes, I think you really need rice vinegar. Rice vinegar has a soft, mild flavor and is useful for making dressings, such as for sushi rice. I also use rice vinegar extensively when I make my own pickles.

Noodles

Like the Chinese and the Italians, we love noodles and use them hot or cold, fried, boiled, or in soups. The two major noodles that are used are soba, buckwheat noodles and udon, a slightly fatter, white noodle. You usually find soba noodles dried but udon come either dried or fresh.

There are many other types of noodles such as somen or harusame but the two basic types that are featured in this book are soba and udon.

Tofu

I cannot believe how unpopular tofu is outside Japan! It is made from soy beans and is one of the most wonderfully versatile ingredients that can be used in so many dishes. I think the problem with most tofu outside Japan is its quality; it is worth trying to find the best—I think the best is Japanese. There are two types, soft/silken or firm/cotton and for most recipes I prefer the soft/silken type.

It is difficult to get fresh tofu outside Japan, so the tofu you will find is usually long-lasting but it will need to be kept refrigerated. The other matter with tofu is how to drain it. It is packaged in water and when opened needs to be drained before use. If a recipe requires the tofu to be well drained before use, I will usually wrap it in paper towel and leave it in a strainer for 30 minutes to 1 hour.

Potato starch

Katakuriko (also called potato starch) is a very useful ingredient. It thickens liquids better than corn starch or standard flour and gives deep-fried foods a lovely crispiness. One of the major sauces in the book, ankake, is made using this ingredient and I cannot imagine it being as successful with a substitute ingredient. A bag of this will last a long time and is worth investing in.

Kombu seaweed (dried kelp)

We use all sorts of seaweed in cooking in Japan but This one is really important because it helps flavor the crucial dashi stock. The seaweed itself looks like real seaweed with rubbery, long leaves. Simply cut it into the lengths required—you will find mention in these recipes of 2in or 4in pieces. Just cut the kombu to size. It needs to be wiped with a damp cloth or lightly washed under cold running water and dried before use because it often has powdery, salty deposits on its surface.

Nori seaweed

For many this is a more familiar ingredient and is the seaweed that is found wrapped around sushi rolls. It is crispy and dry and you use it straight from the package. It can be used to wrap rice balls or sushi rice rolls or it can be shredded and sprinkled on top of dishes. Nori easily absorbs moisture, so try to use it at the last minute to ensure it stays nice and crispy. It is a dried ingredient, so it keeps well in any kitchen cupboard, but to ensure it is crispy when you use it, you should keep an eye on its use-by date and keep any leftover nori in an airtight container. Alternatively, it can be frozen.

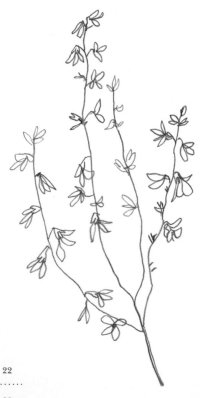

Wasabi

Anyone who has eaten sushi will know wasabi, the ubiquitous fiery green paste dabbed under the raw fish. This Japanese horseradish is mainly grown in the clean running waters of the Izu Penninsula, where I come from. If you go to a good sushi restaurant you will find them using a shark skin grater to make the wasabi paste, but most people these days buy it in tubes or as a powder. If you ever have the opportunity to try fresh wasabi, I strongly urge you to taste it. It is a world apart from that which is sold premade in supermarkets. I would also urge you not to use too much wasabi. It should provide a delicate heat not an overwhelming one.

Shichimi togarashi

Shichimi togarashi is a spicy powder made up of seven different seasonings, including peppers and chili. I use it frequently, sprinkled on top of soups or grilled meat or fish. It has a more interesting flavor than just chili and is worth trying to find as it is always useful.

Ginger, garlic, and superfine sugar

I've included ginger, garlic, and sugar as part of my essential Japanese kitchen cupboard because they are universal ingredients in many of my recipes. Japanese food uses a lot of fresh ginger and I particularly love it. Try to always have a fresh, firm piece of ginger in the kitchen—it will always be useful and can be added to so many dishes. Garlic is also popular and again I would urge you to have a bulb of fresh garlic around to use. Sugar is a basic but important element of Japanese cooking and surprisingly, I think it tastes slightly different from the sugars I have tasted overseas. You can experiment using less and find what suits your taste. Even within Japan there is quite a regional difference in the amount of sugar used. It is possible that the sweetness in these dishes satisfies a need and thereby helps avoid serving up large fattening desserts! Certainly if you look at most Japanese you will find them to be slim and healthy. The sugar may seem unhealthy but if you create a meal with variety and with portions of the size served in Japan you will find it a very balanced way of eating.

Sauces and dressings

One of my most successful books was one with recipes for different sauces and dressings, which are an essential part of the vocabulary in Japanese cuisine. So in addition to the essential ingredients mentioned previously there are also some sauces and dressings that are worth preparing and keeping in your refrigerator.

On the following pages the first three are soy sauce based sauces and are used in many recipes in this book.

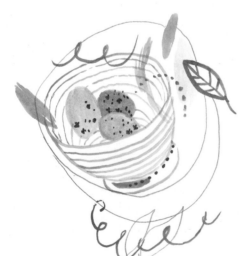

Banno soy sauce

I like to experiment with flavors and I first made this banno soy sauce when my son was very young. I wanted to soften and slightly sweeten the flavor of soy sauce and make it more suitable to add to his favorite food, natto—an ingredient made from fermented soy beans often regarded as quite a taste challenge for the non-Japanese palate.

The mirin and kombu seaweed make this sauce much milder than regular soy sauce and it can be used in its place in many recipes. I often make a large batch and keep it in my fridge.

½ cup mirin
1¼ cups soy sauce
4 inch piece kombu seaweed (dried kelp)

1. Bring the mirin to a boil, then turn down the heat, and cook for 2–3 minutes over low heat to burn off its alcohol content.
2. Take it off the heat and stir in the soy sauce.
3. To remove any excess saltiness from the kombu either lightly wash under running water and then pat dry or gently wipe with a damp cloth. Add to the soy sauce mixture.
4. Leave to stand for a couple of hours, then remove the kombu and refrigerate. It will keep for up to 3 weeks.

Mentsuyu

There are many versions of this classic sauce but this, I believe, is the tastiest. Once made, it can be kept in the refrigerator and used in many Japanese dishes, such as traditional ones using soba or udon noodles or more contemporary ones like my recipe for mixed vegetables in mentsuyu (see page 184).

2 x 4in pieces dried kombu seaweed (dried kelp)
1¼ cups soy sauce
1 cup mirin
scant ¼ cup superfine sugar
2 oz katsuobushi (dried fish flakes)

1. To remove excess saltiness from the kombu either lightly wash under running water then pat dry or wipe with a damp cloth. Then leave to soak in a large saucepan in 3½ cups of water for 30 minutes to 1 hour, depending on the thickness of the kombu.
2. Add the soy sauce, mirin, and sugar to the water and kombu and heat.
3. Just before it comes to a boil, add the katsuobushi.
4. Boil for 2–3 minutes, then take off the heat, cool, and strain.
5. Pour into a bottle or jar and keep refrigerated for up to 1 week. It is delicious as a dressing for salads, such as a rare roast beef salad.

Ponzu soy sauce

In Japan we have a large variety of citrus fruits available, like sudachi or kabosu, most of which are suitable to use when making ponzu soy sauce. This recipe has a lovely fresh aroma that comes from the addition of lemon juice. It can be served with many foods but particularly complements seafood. It can also be made with lime juice.

½ cup mirin
½ cup soy sauce
¼ cup lemon juice
2 inch piece kombu seaweed (dried kelp)

1. Put the mirin in a saucepan and bring to the boil then turn down to a low heat and continue cooking for 2–3 minutes to burn off any alcohol. Then remove from the heat.
2. Add the soy sauce and lemon juice. To remove any excess saltiness from the kombu seaweed either wash it under running water and pat dry or wipe with a damp cloth. Then add to the mixture.
3. Leave to cool then remove the kombu and refrigerate. It can be used for up to a week.

The next two sauces are made from two essential ingredients, sesame and miso. Sesame provides the base for many sauces. Although sesame sauce is easy to buy ready-made in Japan, I like to make my own. I make it throughout the year and keep it in my refrigerator, labeled clearly so I know when it was made and which bottle to use next. It can be used in so many recipes, either as is or with the addition of a drop of dashi stock and sweet vinegar as a salad dressing.

Sesame paste

1 cup toasted sesame seeds
½ cup soy sauce
scant ⅓ cup superfine sugar

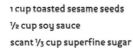

1. Grind ⅔ cup of the sesame seeds in a mortar until they start sticking together, almost like a paste.
2. Put the ground sesame into a bowl, add the soy sauce and sugar, and mix well.
3. Lightly grind the remaining ⅓ cup of sesame seeds in the mortar, being careful not to grind them as finely as the first batch.
4. Add these lightly ground sesame seeds to the sesame, soy, and sugar mixture and blend together well.
5. Put in a container and keep in the refrigerator for 2–3 weeks; after then it will lose its intense flavor, so use it up quickly.

Miso paste

This has a great light flavor. It can be used to marinate meat or fish, added to soups, used for stir-frying, or just as a dipping sauce with crudités. Mixed with a little sweet vinegar or mayonnaise it will transform itself into another dressing that can be used in many other ways. I think the addition of sake and mirin give it an extra richness.

13 oz awase miso (see page 21)
½ cup sake
1 cup mirin
⅓ cup superfine sugar

1. Mix the ingredients together in a saucepan over medium heat.
2. When it comes to a boil, turn the heat down low.
3. Continue cooking for about 20 minutes, stirring as the liquid reduces so that it does not burn, then remove from the heat.
4. When cool, place in a container and keep in the refrigerator for 2–3 weeks.

I have two really useful recipes for sweetened vinegars, one with mirin and other without. These vinegars are used in a variety of recipes but are mainly used for pickling. They are not as sharp and acidic as the pickling vinegars used in other countries.

When preparing a recipe that requires a sweetened vinegar, I will use the version that suits the dish the best. If you use these for preparing sushi rice you should add a little salt.

Sweetened vinegar with mirin

1 cup mirin
1 cup rice vinegar (unseasoned)
2–3 tablespoons superfine sugar
2 teaspoons salt

1. Put the mirin in a small saucepan and heat. When it comes to a boil, turn the heat down low and simmer for 3 minutes, then turn off the heat.
2. Add the vinegar, sugar, and salt in this order to the mirin and stir constantly until the sugar and salt are dissolved.
3. Store in a suitable container in the refrigerator for up to 3–4 weeks.

Sweetened vinegar without mirin

1¼ cups rice vinegar (unseasoned)
scant ¼ cup superfine sugar
1 teaspoon salt

1. Combine the ingredients in a bowl and mix until the sugar and salt have completely dissolved.
2. Store in a suitable container in the refrigerator for up to 3–4 weeks.

I hope that you will enjoy using these recipes as much as I enjoyed making them. I do think that this book will give you the necessary building blocks to make a variety of Japanese dishes and to understand how Japanese cuisine works. I now know, from my own experience, that tackling Japanese cooking is like learning a new language because you need a new "vocabulary" of ingredients and methods. But the pleasure you will get when it all works, when your friends and family enjoy your food, is immense.

I am very proud of this barbecue sauce, which took a lot of trial and error to get the right balance of flavors. It works well with any kind of meat, particularly beef. Before barbecuing, coat the meat with the sauce and after cooking, dip it in again for extra flavor.

Harumi's Barbecue Sauce

MAKES 2 GENEROUS CUPS

½ cup red wine

2 tablespoons honey

heaping ¼ cup superfine sugar

1 cup soy sauce

1 tablespoon awase miso (see page 21)

⅓ cup grated apple

⅓ cup grated onion

2 tablespoons grated garlic

1 tablespoon grated fresh ginger

1–2 tablespoons sesame oil

3 tablespoons ground toasted
   sesame seeds

1. Put the red wine in a small pan and heat. When it comes to a boil, turn the heat down low, letting it simmer gently for about 1 minute to burn off the alcohol content.

2. Add the honey, sugar, soy sauce, and miso to the wine and combine. When it comes to a boil again and the sugar has dissolved, remove from the heat.

3. Let it cool and add the grated apple, onion, garlic, ginger, sesame oil, and ground sesame seeds in this order and mix. The flavor will improve if left overnight. It can be stored in the refrigerator in a container for up to 10 days.

This is a lovely light soup with crispy vegetables and tasty pieces of beef. I found that for the best flavor, the beef should be marinated shortly before it is cooked. I like this particular marinade because it seems to enhance the flavor of the beef. Make sure the vegetables are added just before you are ready to serve the soup—it is important they are not overcooked. The combination of crispy shredded vegetables and the highly seasoned beef is wonderful and the further addition of the shichimi togarashi (Japanese chili pepper) just makes for a great dish. It is a really easy soup for beginners because the flavor comes from the marinade and all that is needed before serving is to check whether it needs more salt.

Beef and Finely Shredded Vegetable Soup

SERVES 4

FOR THE BEEF :

7 oz thinly sliced beef
¼ – ⅓ cup soy sauce
1 tablespoon sake
1–2 tablespoons mirin
1–2 teaspoons superfine sugar
pepper—to season

FOR THE SOUP:

small carrot
large stalk celery
⅔ cup watercress
¾ oz fresh ginger
5 cups dashi stock (see page 19)
salt—to season
shichimi togarashi or chili pepper—
    to taste

1. To marinate the beef: Cut the thinly sliced beef into 1½–2 inch long strips, place in a bowl, and add the soy sauce, sake, mirin, and sugar. Mix together and season with pepper. Set aside to marinate for 10 minutes.

2. To make the soup: Chop the carrot into julienne strips 2½ inches long.

3. Remove any stringy parts from the celery stalk and chop into similar-sized julienne.

4. Trim the stems from the watercress and divide into four.

5. Peel and slice the fresh ginger into fine julienne.

6. Put the dashi stock into a large saucepan over medium heat. Once it has come to a boil, add the beef and the marinade. Skim off any scum that forms on the surface.

7. Add the carrot, celery, ginger, and watercress in this order, then add salt to season. Gently boil for a few minutes, being careful not to let the vegetables overcook—they should still be quite crunchy when you serve them.

8. Serve the soup with some shichimi togarashi or chili powder sprinkled on top.

All supermarkets in Japan sell miso-marinated meats. Although they are convenient, I prefer to make my own miso marinade. For this recipe I like to use a slightly sweet, mild miso paste but I recommend you experiment with different types of miso paste to find the one that suits you. This marinade can be used for any type of meat, fish, or even vegetables. It is best spread on the fresh ingredient, covered in plastic wrap, and then refrigerated for one or two days. This ensures that the subtle flavor of the miso is absorbed. This marinade can be kept in a sealed container in the refrigerator for up to three weeks.

Sirloin Steak in a Miso Marinade

SERVES 4

4 sirloin steaks, each about 1 inch thick

FOR THE MARINADE:
13 oz awase miso paste (see page 29)
½ cup sake
1 cup mirin
⅓ cup superfine sugar
wasabi

1. To make the marinade: Combine all the marinade ingredients in a saucepan and bring to a boil over medium heat.
2. Reduce the heat and continue to stir over a low heat for about 20 minutes, until the sauce thickens, being careful not to let it burn.
3. To prepare the steaks: Spread 2 tablespoons of the marinade on each side of the steaks and cover in plastic wrap. Leave the meat in the refrigerator for no less than 12 hours or overnight.
4. When ready to cook, remove the steaks from the refrigerator and allow to come to room temperature. Remove the excess marinade from the steaks using a spatula. Preheat a grill and sear the steaks quickly on both sides. Turn down the heat and cook according to personal preference. The steaks can be pan-fried, if preferred.
5. Slice the steaks and serve with grilled vegetables and wasabi.

There is a lovely combination of textures and flavors to this dish. The dressing is one that can be used for other salads and can easily be adjusted according to personal taste. Shredding the chicken may seem unnecessary but I think it makes the salad taste lighter and airier. In fact, I will often prepare and cook extra chicken when I am making this dish and I will shred it all and freeze what I don't immediately use; it is very useful to have it in the freezer to use in salads or soups in the future.

Chicken and Celery Salad

SERVES 4

5 stalks celery (about 10 oz)

10 oz skinless chicken breasts
    or mini fillets

½ teaspoon grated garlic

1–2 tablespoons light soy sauce

½ tablespoon sunflower or
    vegetable oil (optional)

FOR THE DRESSING:

heaping ⅓ cup mayonnaise

1 tablespoon chicken stock

1–2 tablespoons white wine

light soy sauce—to taste

wasabi—to taste

salt and pepper—to season

pepper—to serve

1. Remove any stringy parts of the celery. Chop into strips 2 inches long. Put into iced water for a couple of minutes to crisp, then drain.

2. Remove any gristle from the chicken then season by mixing the garlic with the light soy sauce and marinate for 5–6 minutes.

3. Cook the chicken in a nonstick skillet until it is just cooked through. If using a regular skillet, use a little oil when cooking the chicken.

4. When cool, shred the chicken into thin strips by hand and mix with the celery.

5. To make the dressing: Mix the mayonnaise with the chicken stock and white wine, then add the light soy sauce and wasabi, according to personal taste, and finally season with salt and pepper.

6. Dress the chicken and celery and put in a serving dish. Sprinkle pepper on top and serve. Please take care with the presentation of this salad, fluffing it up as much as possible.

This recipe reminds me of my father. He said he didn't like chicken but when I cooked this for him, I think he changed his mind. It soon became one his favorite dishes. I loved cooking it for him and seeing the pleasure it gave him. It is also popular with my readers. I first introduced this recipe in one of my magazines almost 20 years ago and I still hear people comment on it. I hope you too will enjoy this delicious mixture of crispy chicken with a tasty hot leek sauce.

Deep-fried Chicken with a Leek Sauce

SERVES 4

1 lb boneless chicken thighs
    with skin on
½ tablespoon soy sauce
½ tablespoon sake
potato starch or cornstarch—
    for coating the chicken
sunflower or vegetable oil—
    for deep-frying

FOR THE LEEK SAUCE:
½–1 leek
½ cup soy sauce
1 tablespoon sake
2 tablespoons rice vinegar,
    unseasoned
1½ tablespoons superfine sugar
½ tablespoon sunflower or
    vegetable oil
1 red chili, without seeds,
    roughly chopped

1. To make the leek sauce: Pierce the leek randomly with a sharp knife and then chop finely. This method makes it easier to mince.
2. Mix the soy sauce, sake, rice vinegar, and sugar together in a bowl. Heat the oil in a skillet and lightly sauté the minced leek and the red chili. Then add the soy sauce, the sake, rice vinegar, and sugar to the pan, stirring constantly. When the sugar has dissolved take off the heat and set aside.
3. Pierce the chicken skin with a fork, cut any large pieces in half, and marinate for 5 minutes in the soy sauce and sake.
4. Remove the chicken from the marinade and coat thoroughly with potato starch.
5. For the best results, the chicken should be at room temperature before deep-frying.
6. Deep-fry the chicken at a medium-high temperature (340°F). Make sure each piece is completely immersed in the oil so it cooks on the inside while remaining crispy on the outside.
7. Remove when golden brown, drain, and cut into bite-sized pieces just before serving. Place on a serving dish and cover with the leek sauce.

Fried chicken seems to be popular all around the world, with each country having its own style. I love all kinds of fried chicken, Western or Asian. This recipe is very easy and is a good introduction to Japanese fried chicken. You will be amazed at how many of these small treats you, your family, and your friends will eat.

Karaage Chicken

SERVES 4

1¼lb boneless chicken thighs with
    skin on
2 tablespoons garlic and ginger soy
    sauce (see below)
salt—to season
½ cup potato starch or corn starch
⅓ cup all-purpose flour
sunflower or vegetable oil—
    for deep-frying
lemon or lime, shichimi togarashi or
    chili pepper, mayonnaise—
    to serve

FOR THE GARLIC AND GINGER
    SOY SAUCE:
4 fat cloves garlic
2 oz fresh ginger
1 cup soy sauce

1. To make the garlic and ginger soy sauce: Peel the garlic and ginger, slice thinly and add to the soy sauce. Leave for half a day to produce a deep flavor.
2. Cut the chicken in small, bite-sized pieces. Completely cover with the ginger and garlic soy sauce and marinate for 5–10 minutes, then season with salt to taste.
3. Combine the potato starch and all-purpose flour and completely coat each piece of chicken then deep-fry in very hot oil (356°F).
4. When the chicken is a golden color, cooked through, and very crispy, remove from the oil and drain on a rack or on some paper towel.
5. Put each piece of chicken on a small wooden skewer and serve with lemon, shichimi togarashi, and mayonnaise.

Yakitori is very popular with all age groups and is great for entertaining, especially if the weather is good enough for a barbecue. These chicken skewers are often served to accompany drinks and can be found served in pubs all over Japan. They are very versatile and can be prepared with just salt and pepper but I like serving them with my own teriyaki sauce, which can also be used with beef, pork, and salmon. Try it and see—it's really delicious.

Yakitori

MAKES 12 SKEWERS

1 lb boneless chicken thighs
   with skin on
6 baby leeks
12 bamboo skewers
sunflower or vegetable oil
½ cup teriyaki sauce (see below)
salt and pepper—to taste

FOR THE TERIYAKI SAUCE
½ cup soy sauce
½ cup mirin
4 tablespoons superfine sugar

1. To prepare the teriyaki sauce: Put the soy sauce, mirin, and superfine sugar into a small saucepan and gently cook for 20 minutes. Skim the surface of any scum and set aside.

2. Cut the chicken into 1 inch-square pieces. Wash the leeks, dry and then cut into 1¾ inch lengths. Soak the bamboo skewers in water for a few minutes to stop them from burning during cooking.

3. Thread the chicken and leeks onto the skewers, alternating between the chicken and the leek pieces.

4. Put a little oil into a large skillet and when well-heated, add the skewers and fry until nicely browned and cooked through. You can also cook these skewers on a barbecue or simply broil them.

5. When the chicken and leek skewers are ready to serve, coat them in the teriyaki sauce or alternatively sprinkle with salt and pepper. Arrange on a large plate and serve.

My daughter always loved chicken and so I would often prepare this dish for her to take to school in her bento box. These fillets are quick and easy to prepare and can be eaten hot or cold. Ovens are still fairly unusual in Japan, so this dish is normally cooked in what we call an oven toaster—smaller than a real oven but very convenient.

Mini Chicken Fillets with Mayonnaise

SERVES 2–4

4 skinless mini chicken fillets
½ teaspoon light soy sauce
some grated garlic—to taste
2 tablespoons mayonnaise
4 tablespoons grated Parmesan
 cheese

1. Remove any gristle from the chicken fillets. Put on a plate, cover in the light soy sauce and garlic and marinate for 2–3 minutes.
2. Put the chicken on a baking pan lined with parchment paper and spread the mayonnaise evenly over the fillet. Finish by sprinkling the Parmesan on top.
3. Heat the oven to 450°F and cook for 7–8 minutes, until browned.

Some recipes are fantastic for sharing and creating a wonderful atmosphere; recipes that not only taste good but also make people feel good. This one for simmered pork in crêpes is one that I have always found brings people together. Even people who have only just met will get chatty while sharing this dish. It is popular with all age groups and I love it because it can be prepared in advance, allowing me to take part in the fun. I will sometimes use fried chicken instead of the pork; it works just as well.

Simmered Pork in Crêpes

SERVES 4–6

1½ lb pork shoulder

sunflower or vegetable oil—
    for frying

½ cup soy sauce

¼ cup sake

1 tablespoon superfine sugar

1 leek or 2 scallions

a piece of fresh ginger, peeled and
    lightly crushed

4 hard-cooked eggs, peeled

FOR THE CRÊPES:

heaping ¾ cup all-purpose flour

1 teaspoon superfine sugar

a little salt

1 tablespoon sunflower or
    vegetable oil

TO SERVE:

1 cucumber, sliced into julienne

2 leeks or 4 scallions, sliced into
    julienne, washed and dried

a small bag of mixed salad leaves

fresh mint, watercress, basil,
    cilantro

some miso paste (see page 29)

1. To cook the pork: Cut the joint in half, which will help it cook more quickly.
2. Put a little oil in a deep, heavy saucepan and place on medium heat. Add the pork and brown it on all sides. Remove any excess oil from the pan with paper towel.
3. Add the soy sauce, sake, and sugar and just enough water to cover the meat. Add the green stem of the leek and the crushed ginger.
4. Turn up the heat and bring to a boil then, after a few minutes, skim the surface of any scum, reduce the heat and cover with a drop lid (a lid of aluminum foil slightly smaller than the size of the rim of the saucepan that sits inside the pan on top of the meat). Simmer for about 1 hour, skimming the surface and turning the meat occasionally. Add the hard-cooked eggs about 45 minutes into the cooking time to ensure they do not overcook but that they have enough time to absorb the flavors.
5. To make the crêpes: Mix the flour, sugar, salt and 1 cup of water together in a bowl then add the vegetable oil. Leave to stand for a few minutes.
6. Heat a little oil in a nonstick skillet. Pour a thin layer of the mixture into the skillet to make a crêpe. This amount of mixture should make 10–12 thin crêpes.
7. When the pork is cooked and the broth has thickened, remove the eggs, cut them in half, and slice the pork into bite-sized pieces.
8. Create a visual feast, arranging the pork slices and egg halves with the julienned cucumbers, leeks, herbs, and crêpes on serving plates.
9. Let everyone help themselves to make their own wraps filled with vegetables, pork, and eggs and spice them up by dipping into the miso sauce.

Tsukune is the word for a ground meat patty, a sort of Japanese mini hamburger. They can be made with any combination of ground meat, though the usual "ground meat" on sale in Japan is a mixture of pork and beef. A good way to introduce more vegetables into your diet is by adding chopped vegetables, such as onion, leeks, carrots, shiitake mushrooms, or celery, to the ground meat. You can serve these tsukune with a teriyaki sauce or with a miso dressing or simply with salt and pepper. You can also change the shape from a burger shape to a sausage. It is a very useful dish, popular with all families.

Japanese Tsukune with Teriyaki Sauce

SERVES 4

small onion (about 4 oz), peeled
1 stalk celery
10 oz ground meat
salt and pepper—to season
1 medium egg
2 tablespoons all-purpose flour
5–6 basil leaves

FOR THE TERIYAKI SAUCE:

½ cup soy sauce
½ cup mirin
4 tablespoons superfine sugar

sunflower or vegetable oil—
    for frying
shichimi togarashi or chili pepper,
sansho (or szechwan pepper) and
sudachi wedges (or lemon)—to taste

1. To make the teriyaki sauce: Combine the soy sauce, mirin, and sugar in a pan and slowly bring to a boil. Turn the heat down low and simmer for about 20 minutes, until it has thickened. Skim the surface of any scum if necessary and set aside.

2. To make the tsukune: Roughly chop the onion. Remove any stringy parts from the celery and chop it roughly.

3. Put all the ingredients, except the basil, into a bowl and knead to combine well. Finally, chop the basil into tiny pieces and add to the mixture. It is important to add the basil at the last minute so it retains its color.

4. Shape the mixture into rounds about 2 inches in diameter. Drizzle a little oil in a nonstick skillet and heat. When hot, add the tsukune and cook until nicely browned on both sides.

5. Take the cooked tsukune, dip them in the teriyaki sauce while still hot, and sprinkle with shichimi togarashi and sansho according to your own preference. Serve with sudachi or lemon wedges on the side.

Tonkatsu is popular with everyone but especially with men—it has become one of Japanese mens' favorite dishes. The tonkatsu steaks are best served piping hot on a bed of crispy, julienned cabbage. To make the cabbage really crisp, I like to cut it into fine strips and then soak it in iced water. Tonkatsu is so popular that I always make extra, in a variety of sizes, and freeze them for those occasions when I don't have much time to cook or I have more people to feed than anticipated. If you freeze the tonkatsu uncooked you can take it straight from the freezer and deep fry, though the cooking takes a little longer.

Tonkatsu

SERVES 4

13 oz green cabbage
4 x 5 oz pork shoulder steaks,
    each about 1in thick
salt and pepper—to season
flour—for coating
1 medium egg, beaten
breadcrumbs—for coating
sunflower or vegetable oil—
    for deep-frying
tonkatsu sauce and mustard—to taste

1. Cut the cabbage into fine strips and soak in a large bowl of iced water for about 5 minutes, to crisp. Drain and put in a plastic food bag and refrigerate until ready to serve the tonkatsu.

2. Make a few small cuts around the edges of each pork steak so they will cook without shrinking. Season with salt and pepper.

3. Cover each pork steak in flour, then dip in beaten egg and coat with breadcrumbs.

4. Heat the oil for deep-frying in a deep saucepan. Check the temperature by dropping a few breadcrumbs into the oil—if they float immediately, it is at the correct temperature (340°F).

5. Deep-fry each pork steak on medium heat until they are cooked through and golden brown. When cooked, drain on a rack or some paper towels to remove any excess oil. Slice the pork into bite-sized pieces and serve with a large helping of crispy shredded cabbage on the side.
It is normally served with a pat of mustard and some tonkatsu sauce. This sauce is usually store-bought and I would recommend you try to find it from a Japanese supermarket, because it is very hard to replicate. Worcestershire sauce is an acceptable accompaniment if you cannot find tonkatsu sauce.

The word katsudon comes from tonkatsu, a deep-fried pork steak, and donburi, the word for a bowl of rice with an added ingredient on top. A typical katsudon is a bowl of hot rice with a tonkatsu steak on top but the tonkatsu is given extra flavor by being cooked in a special sauce and covered with a delicious egg topping. This is really popular family food, especially for hungry youngsters.

Katsudon

SERVES 1

1 cooked tonkatsu pork steak (see page 59)

small onion (about 2 oz), peeled

1–2 medium eggs—to taste

½ cup dashi stock (see page 19)

2 tablespoons soy sauce

1 tablespoon mirin

1 tablespoon sugar

a bowl of hot cooked Japanese sushi rice—approximately ¾ cup

1. Cut the tonkatsu pork steak into 6 bite-sized pieces. Slice the onion thinly. In a bowl, lightly beat the eggs together.
2. Put the dashi, soy sauce, mirin, and sugar into a small saucepan and cook over medium heat until the sugar dissolves.
3. Add the onion and cook until it starts to soften, then add the tonkatsu pork steak and cook until heated through.
4. Pour the beaten egg on top of the tonkatsu pork steak and leave to cook—do not mix it in. When the egg looks almost cooked, cover the pan with a lid, turn off the heat, and allow it to absorb the flavors.
5. Carefully tip the tonkatsu pork steak, the onion, and the remaining liquid onto a bowl of hot rice and eat immediately.

This classic recipe is very easy to make, but it is also easy to do badly. Take care of the details and the dish will be outstanding. With very thin slices of pork, such as are used here, it is essential that they are cooked quickly at a high temperature, otherwise the dish will become watery. It is also important not to soak the pork in the soy sauce mixture for too long or the meat will become tough. I am sure this dish, with its wonderful combination of soy, mirin, ginger, and pork, will be popular with everyone who tries it.

Ginger Pork

SERVES 4

13 oz pork shoulder

11½ oz bok choy

1 tablespoon grated fresh ginger

⅓ cup soy sauce

¼ cup mirin

sunflower or vegetable oil— for frying

salt and pepper—to season

1. Briefly freeze the pork as this will make it easier to slice. Slice the pork as thinly as possible, then wrap the slices in plastic wrap and tenderize by hitting with a rolling pin.

2. Remove the plastic wrap. It is important to ensure that the pork is at room temperature before cooking.

3. Separate the white stem from the green leaf of the bok choy. Cut the stems lengthwise and the leaves in half.

4. Blend the soy sauce and mirin together, add the grated ginger, and mix to combine.

5. Put a little oil in a skillet over high heat. Stir in the bok choy stems then the leaves and stir-fry for 1 minute. Season with salt and pepper and arrange on the plates that will be used for the pork.

6. Dip the pork slices into the soy and ginger mixture and quickly brown in the hot skillet. Serve with the bok choy.

This dish is something of a tradition in my household. It is easy to prepare, only needing soy sauce for seasoning, and makes use of wonderful ingredients like ginger, garlic, and Japanese leeks. It is a great dish that can be rustled up quickly if guests drop in unexpectedly. I usually serve it with white rice and if there are any leftovers, they don't last long in our house.

Green Beans with Ground Pork

SERVES 4

3 cups green beans

small leek (about 2oz)

½ oz fresh ginger, peeled

2 fat cloves garlic

sunflower or vegetable oil—
    for frying

7 oz ground pork

2–3 tablespoons soy sauce

sliced fresh or dried red chilies—
    to taste

sesame oil—to taste

1. Prepare the green beans, lightly cook in boiling water, then rinse under cold running water.
2. Drain the beans, pat them dry, and cut diagonally into bite-sized pieces.
3. Finely chop the leek, ginger, and garlic.
4. Put a little oil in a skillet over high heat. Add the chopped leek, ginger, and garlic, allowing the flavors to infuse in the oil, then add the ground pork and stir-fry.
5. Add the green beans, then add soy sauce and red chili to taste.
6. Continue to cook until the beans have heated through. Add a little sesame oil to taste and serve with hot white rice.

I learned how to cook this recipe from my grandmother. It is a very versatile soup—the ingredients can be changed according to what is available in the supermarket or what you have in your fridge. You can use other types of fish such as mackerel or sea bream, or other vegetables like eggplant. Here I am using daikon, a Japanese white radish. It is a lovely vegetable to use both raw in salads or as it is here, gently stewed. Be careful when you add the fish to the soup. It can become lumpy if you add too much at once.

Halibut and Daikon Soup

SERVES 4

7 oz halibut fillet

10 oz daikon (mooli or Japanese white radish)

3½ cups dashi stock (see page 19)

2 tablespoons mirin

2 tablespoons soy sauce

1 tablespoon light soy sauce

salt—to season

shichimi togarashi (or chili pepper) or grated fresh ginger—to taste

1. Remove any skin from the fish and check for bones. Mince the flesh with a knife then grind it in a mortar to make a really smooth paste.
2. Peel the daikon and chop into rounds ¾ inches thick, then cut into quarters.
3. Pour the dashi stock into a saucepan and heat. Add the daikon pieces and cook until softened, then add the soy sauce, the light soy sauce, and the mirin.
4. Take some of the hot soup stock and add it little by little to the fish paste in the mortar, stirring as it is added. Then carefully stir the fish paste mixture from the mortar into the soup stock in the saucepan and simmer gently for 1–2 minutes.
5. Taste and season with a little salt. Serve hot with shichimi togarashi or a little grated ginger on top.

This recipe, called saba soboro in Japanese, is another family standard. This particular version is one that my mother gave to me. I too have been cooking this for my children from when they were very small; we all enjoy the taste of fresh mackerel mixed with vegetables and it is great that it is so healthy, too. I have developed a trick to remove the flesh from the mackerel fillet, important for this recipe: I use a spoon and gently scrape the flesh away from the skin. Everyone I know who has seen me do this is amazed at how quickly and easily it can be done. This dish works well as a main course or in a bento box.

Flaked Mackerel with Vegetables

SERVES 4

12 oz fresh mackerel fillets

1½ cup shiitake mushrooms

½ oz ginger, peeled

medium-sized carrot (about 5 oz)

small onion, peeled

1 tablespoon sunflower or
   vegetable oil

1 tablespoon sake

1 tablespoon superfine sugar

2 tablespoons mirin

2–3 tablespoons soy sauce

1 tablespoon awase miso (see page 21)

1. Remove any visible bones from the mackerel fillets and scoop the mackerel flesh from the skin from head to tail, using a spoon. Roughly break up the flesh and set aside.
2. Trim and dice the mushrooms.
3. Finely chop the ginger. Peel and dice the carrot and onion.
4. Heat the oil in a skillet. Add the ginger and mackerel flesh and brown slightly. When the mackerel starts to change color, add the carrot, onion, and shiitake mushrooms, in this order.
5. Finally, add the sake, sugar, mirin, soy sauce, and miso. Keep stirring until most of the liquid has been absorbed. Serve with hot white rice.

Salmon is usually cooked as a fillet but I like to mince it—it can be used like this in many different recipes. Here I mix it with shrimp, but equally you can replace them with chopped pork or chicken. I like to leave the onions in quite large pieces because they give the fish cakes an extra bite and I love serving them with lots of fresh shredded ginger on top. You will be amazed how different really finely shredded ginger tastes—be brave and try these delicious fish cakes with more shredded ginger than you would usually take.

Salmon and Shrimp Fish Cakes

MAKES 18 SMALL FISH CAKES

12 oz salmon

4 oz peeled raw shrimp

small onion

1 tablespoon sake

salt and pepper—to season

sunflower or vegetable oil—
    for frying

ponzu soy sauce

some finely shredded fresh ginger—
    to garnish

FOR THE PONZU SOY SAUCE.

½ cup mirin

½ cup soy sauce

¼ cup lemon juice

2 inch piece kombu seaweed
    (dried kelp), wiped of
    any salty deposits

1. To make the ponzu soy sauce: In a small saucepan, bring the mirin to a boil, then reduce the heat and cook for a further 2–3 minutes over low heat to burn off the alcohol. Remove from the heat and add the soy sauce, lemon juice, and kombu and leave to cool.

2. Remove any skin or bones from the salmon and finely mince.

3. Devein the shrimp and chop finely. Both the salmon and shrimp should resemble ground meat.

4. Chop the onion into pieces ½–¾ inches in size.

5. Put the salmon and shrimp into a bowl, mix well, then add the onion and mix again. Add the sake, some salt and pepper to season, and combine thoroughly.

6. Shape the mixture into small fish cakes, each one being around 2 inches in diameter.

7. Heat a little oil in a large skillet and when hot place the fish cakes in the pan, allowing them to brown well before turning them over.

8. Once cooked, place on a large plate and drizzle over the ponzu soy sauce and garnish with some shredded fresh ginger on top of each fish cake.

This traditional nanbanzuke dish is a favorite of my husband and I find that I make it frequently throughout the year. Nanbanzuke is the Japanese name for this delicious combination of dashi stock, sweet vinegar, lemon, and chili. It is a wonderful sauce that can be used with meat or fish, but is especially good with salmon and is best served with lots of healthy vegetables. The cooked salmon will keep well in the refrigerator for three to four days.

Salmon Nanbanzuke

SERVES 4

2 stalks celery

small carrot (about 3 oz), peeled

½ oz fresh ginger, peeled

2 red chilies

small onion (about 3½ oz), peeled

1¼ lb salmon fillets
    (approximately 4 fillets)

salt and pepper—to season

all-purpose flour —
    for coating the fish

sunflower or vegetable oil—
    for deep-frying

1 lime, sliced

FOR THE NANBANZUKE SAUCE:

1 cup dashi stock (see page 19)

¼ cup soy sauce

⅓ cup rice vinegar, unseasoned

4 tablespoons superfine sugar

juice from ½–1 lemon

salt—to taste

1. To make the nanbanzuke sauce: Combine the dashi stock, soy sauce, rice vinegar, sugar, and lemon juice in a large bowl and mix well. Add salt to taste.

2. Remove any stringy parts from the celery and chop it and the carrots into 2 inch julienne strips. Cut the ginger into thin matchsticks. Carefully remove the seeds from the chili and slice finely into small rings. Finely slice the onion.

3. Prepare the salmon by cutting into 1½ inch square pieces. Season with a little salt and pepper and dust with flour.

4. Heat enough oil to cover the salmon in a heavy saucepan and when it is very hot, deep-fry the salmon.

5. When just cooked and crispy, remove the salmon from the pan with a slotted spoon to drain off any excess oil and place in the nanbanzuke sauce to marinate. This should be done while still hot so the salmon absorbs the rich flavors of the sauce.

6. Add the celery, carrot, ginger, chili, onion, and sliced lime to the salmon, cover and marinate for a minimum of 30 minutes.

7. To serve, pile a little of the celery, carrot, ginger, chili, onion, and sliced lime on top of each salmon piece.

This simple tasty dish can be prepared with almost any type of fish. It can also be made with any of your favorite ingredients, such as ginger, garlic, or leeks. Remember to add the fish after the liquids have come to a boil to help reduce the odor and ensure the best flavor. Serve with piping hot rice and a bowl of soup; any soup is a good match.

Simmered Sea Bream

SERVES 4

1 lb sea bream fillet with skin on
½ cup sake
½ cup mirin
⅓ cup soy sauce
3 tablespoons superfine sugar
1¼ oz fresh ginger, peeled and
    thinly sliced

1. Prepare the fish by cutting it into four pieces.
2. Gently heat the sake, mirin, soy, sugar and ¼ cup water in a medium-sized saucepan. When the sugar has dissolved, bring to a boil. Add the fish fillets, skin-side down to prevent the skin from shrinking.
3. Add the sliced ginger and reduce the heat. Make a drop lid from some aluminum foil (it should fit tightly inside the saucepan and be placed on top of the fish), and allow to simmer for a few minutes.
4. When the fillets are cooked on the skin side, turn them over and continue cooking until the liquid has reduced by half.
5. Turn off the heat and leave to stand for a while, so the fish can absorb the extra liquid, then serve.

The term tataki is used to describe a method of cooking tuna and beef that involves searing the outside, leaving the inside rare. I think this is the best way to ensure that you taste the real flavor of the ingredient. This recipe also works well with beef.

Tuna Tataki Salad

SERVES 4

8 oz daikon (mooli or Japanese
     white radish)
10 basil leaves
2 tablespoons sunflower or
     vegetable oil
2 fat cloves garlic, finely sliced
14½ oz sashimi-quality tuna
salt and pepper—to season
wasabi and banno soy sauce or
     ponzu soy sauce—to serve

FOR THE BANNO SOY SAUCE:
½ cup mirin
1¼ cups soy sauce
4 inch piece kombu seaweed (dried
     kelp), wiped of any salty deposits

1. To make banno soy sauce: In a small saucepan, bring the mirin to a boil, then reduce the heat and cook for a further 2–3 minutes over low heat to burn off the alcohol. Remove from the heat and add the soy sauce and kombu. Cool and refrigerate.

2. Peel the daikon and chop into fine 2 inch-long julienne strips. Place in iced water to crisp. Drain and dry. Roughly shred the basil leaves. Mix the daikon and basil together.

3. Add the oil to a skillet and heat. Meanwhile, season the tuna with salt and pepper. When the pan is hot, add the sliced garlic and fry until slightly crispy, being careful because it can easily burn. This gives the oil a wonderful aroma. When cooked, remove the garlic with a slotted spoon and set aside.

4. Put the tuna into the hot, garlic-infused oil in the skillet. Cook quickly, crisping both sides but being careful not to overcook— the inside of the tuna should stay rare.

5. Cut the tuna into 1 inch-wide slices and place on a serving plate. Dress with a mix of the julienned daikon, basil leaves, and cooked garlic chips.

6. Prepare a small plate per person with a pat of wasabi and a little banno soy sauce or ponzu soy sauce for dipping.

Ankake is a typical Japanese sauce and can be served with a variety of ingredients. The sauce is made by thickening a seasoned dashi stock with a potato starch and water mix—if you cannot find potato starch you can use corn starch but you will need to make adjustments to the quantities, because it is not as strong a thickening agent as potato starch. Ankake style sauces are the backbone of many Japanese housewives' recipes—they are very suitable to serve as a donburi (on rice).

Shrimp and Chicken Ankake Donburi

SERVES 4

8 oz boneless chicken thighs
    with skin on

3½ oz peeled raw shrimp

salt and pepper—to season

sake—to marinate

1 cup fresh shiitake mushrooms

small onion (about 4oz), peeled

7 oz bok choy leaves

3 tablespoons soy sauce

1 tablespoon sake

1 tablespoon mirin

1 tablespoon superfine sugar

½ teaspoon salt

1²/₃ cups dashi stock (see page 19)

1 tablespoon sunflower or
    vegetable oil—for frying

the green stem of a leek

1½ oz fresh ginger, peeled and halved

3 fat cloves fresh garlic,
    lightly crushed

2 tablespoons potato starch or
    corn starch mixed with
    2 tablespoons cold water

3¼ cups hot cooked rice

1. Cut the chicken into 1 inch-square pieces and devein the shrimp. In separate bowls, season both the chicken and the shrimp with a little sake, salt, and pepper.
2. Clean the mushrooms and trim the stalks. Finely slice them, cutting them on the diagonal.
3. Chop the onion lengthwise, then into wedges and then cut the wedges in half.
4. Prepare the bok choy first by separating the leafy parts from the stems, cutting the stems in half lengthwise and then further chopping them into 2 inch-long pieces. Cut the leaves into pieces of around 2 inches in size.
5. Add the soy sauce, sake, mirin, sugar, and salt to the dashi stock, mix together thoroughly, and set aside.
6. Heat the oil in a skillet. When hot, add the leek, ginger, and garlic, in that order, and cook until you can smell their aroma. Then add the chicken and the shrimp, followed by the mushrooms, onion, and bok choy.
7. Add the dashi stock mixture. When it comes to a boil, stir in the potato starch and water mix to thicken the sauce.
8. Discard the ginger, leek, and garlic. Serve the ankake on hot cooked rice in individual serving bowls.

I think most countries have their own version of shrimp in breadcrumbs; it seems to be a universally popular combination. We often eat giant shrimp dipped in a tempura batter or in breadcrumbs, as ebi fry, but one day I found that I could only find small shrimp so I created this dish. By taking the shrimp, cutting them up and making them into small, almost dumpling shapes, you can make the most fantastic crispy, but moist, shrimp in breadcrumbs.

Shrimp in Crispy Breadcrumbs

SERVES 4

6 oz raw peeled shrimp

1 medium egg

heaping ⅓ cup all-purpose flour

salt and pepper—to season

breadcrumbs—to coat the shrimp

sunflower or vegetable oil—
    for deep-frying

grated fresh ginger and soy sauce or
    ponzu soy sauce—to serve

1. Wash and devein the shrimp then dry them with paper towel.
2. Beat the egg, add the flour, and mix well.
3. Cut each shrimp into three pieces and season with salt and pepper.
4. Take three shrimp pieces and roll them into a ball and lightly flatten.
5. Carefully dip the shrimp ball into the egg and flour mixture and then cover with breadcrumbs. You can always reshape, if they start to fall apart.
6. Heat the oil to about 350°F and deep-fry the shrimp until golden brown and cooked through.
7. Remove the shrimp balls from the pan and drain on a rack or paper towel to drain off any excess oil.
8. Serve hot with soy sauce or ponzu soy sauce mixed with a little grated ginger.

I serve scallops in many different ways, raw as sashimi, fried, sautéed, or grilled. I like the simplicity of this recipe and enjoy eating the juicy scallops hot from the grill, sprinkled with shichimi togarashi and sandwiched between crispy nori seaweed.

Scallops with Nori Seaweed

SERVES 4

7 oz fresh scallops, without the coral

¼–⅓ cup banno soy sauce or regular soy sauce

sunflower or vegetable oil — for frying

nori seaweed

shichimi togarashi or chili pepper— to taste

FOR THE BANNO SOY SAUCE:

½ cup mirin

1¼ cups soy sauce

4 inch piece kombu seaweed (dried kelp), wiped of any salty deposits

1. To make the banno soy sauce: In a small saucepan, bring the mirin to a boil, then reduce the heat to low and cook for a further 2–3 minutes to burn off the alcohol. Remove from the heat and add the soy sauce and kombu. Cool and refrigerate.

2. Put the scallops in a bowl and marinate in the banno soy sauce for 2–3 minutes.

3. Heat a little oil in a skillet and fry the scallops evenly on both sides.

4. When browned, sprinkle some shichimi togarashi on top.

5. Remove from the pan and arrange on a serving plate and sandwich each scallop between pieces of nori—one underneath and another on top. Eat before the nori seaweed loses its crispiness.

I know there is some resistance to deep-frying but I feel that the key to good health is balance. If you only eat deep-fried foods, it would be very unhealthy but occasionally, as part of a meal, I don't think it does you much harm. These scallops are very popular with my family and guests who enjoy the mixture of Italian and Japanese flavors.

Deep-fried Scallops with Mozzarella

SERVES 4

12 large scallops without the coral
1 ball of buffalo mozzarella
12 fresh basil leaves
salt and pepper—to season
1 medium egg, beaten
all-purpose flour—
    to coat the scallops
breadcrumbs—to coat the scallops
sunflower or vegetable oil—
    for deep-frying
lemon wedges, ponzu soy sauce,
    shichimi togarashi, or chili
    pepper—to serve

1. Cut each scallop in half horizontally. Slice the mozzarella into 12 pieces of approximately the same thickness as the scallop halves.
2. Put a slice of mozzarella and a basil leaf in between 2 scallop halves. Season with a little salt and pepper.
3. Coat each scallop and mozzarella "sandwich" with flour, dip into the beaten egg, and then cover in breadcrumbs.
4. Heat enough oil to cover the scallops to 350°F and when hot carefully put in the scallops and deep-fry until golden brown and crispy. Drain on a rack or on some paper towel to remove any excess oil.
5. Serve hot with wedges of lemon, ponzu soy sauce, and shichimi togarashi.

When we were taking the photographs for this book, this recipe was one of the most popular with everyone. It is a very simple dish but has a complexity of flavors that may be new to people who have just been introduced to Japanese food. It is a popular recipe in Japan. The combination of the grilled, lightly salted fish with rice prepared with dashi stock and a variety of other flavors makes for a subtle but exciting mix. Here I have used sea bream but you can use most varieties of white fish just as easily.

Rice Cooked with Sea Bream

SERVES 4

8–10 oz sea bream fillet with skin on
salt—to season
11 oz uncooked Japanese sushi rice
1 tablespoon light soy sauce
1 tablespoon mirin
1 tablespoon sake
1½ cups dashi stock (see page 19)

1. Sprinkle both sides of the sea bream fillet with salt. Grill the skin until it is nicely browned then turn the fillet over and grill until lightly cooked.
2. When the fillet is cool enough to handle, carefully remove any bones.
3. Wash the rice in cold water until the water becomes clear and then drain and leave in a strainer for about 10–15 minutes.
4. Mix the light soy sauce, mirin, sake, and a pinch of salt together in a large liquid measuring cup. Add enough dashi stock to make up to 1⅔ cups of liquid.
5. Put the rice in a heavy saucepan. Place the sea bream on top of the rice and carefully pour the dashi mix into the saucepan—try not to pour it onto the fish.
6. Put a lid on the saucepan and place over high heat. When it comes to a boil, turn the heat down low and cook for 10–12 minutes, after which turn off the heat and leave for a further 10 minutes with the lid on.
7. Remove the lid. Roughly mix the flesh of the grilled sea bream with the rice and serve in bowls.

This beautifully colored dish can be found in all Japanese households and is particularly popular as a bento box. It is a recipe that will remind most Japanese of their childhood. I really enjoy making this dish, taking the time to ensure that the three different toppings are beautifully placed on top of the rice to make it look really attractive. It is a recipe that is complicated only in as much as you need to prepare four different elements and so you need to be well organized before you begin. I find that you can give the rice an extra special flavor if you use the stock from cooking the ground meat to cook the rice.

Three Toppings Rice

SERVES 4

FOR THE RICE

11 oz uncooked Japanese sushi rice

1 cup dashi stock (see page 19)

2 tablespoons soy sauce

1 tablespoon sake

1 tablespoon mirin

1 cup green beans

salt—to season

FOR THE GROUND CHICKEN.

10 oz boneless chicken thighs
    with skin on, ground

scant ¼ cup soy sauce

2 tablespoons mirin

2 tablespoons superfine sugar

1 tablespoon sake

FOR THE SCRAMBLED EGG:

4 medium eggs

1½–2 tablespoons superfine sugar

1 tablespoon sake

salt—to season

1. Wash the rice thoroughly in cold water, drain, and leave in a strainer for 10–15 minutes before cooking.

2. To cook the chicken: This is a two-stage process. First combine the dashi stock, soy sauce, sake, and mirin for cooking the rice in a saucepan and heat. When it comes to a boil, add the ground chicken and cook for a few minutes before straining the chicken. Reserve the liquid to use for cooking the rice, and leave to cool.

3. To cook the rice: Put the liquid used to cook the chicken into a large liquid measuring cup. If necessary, add more dashi stock until there is a total of 1⅔ cups of liquid. Season with a little salt.

4. Put the washed rice and the dashi stock mixture into a heavy saucepan over medium heat, cover with a lid, and bring to a boil. Then reduce the heat and simmer for 10–12 minutes. Then turn off the heat and leave for 10 minutes with the lid on.

5. While the rice is cooking, put the chicken in another saucepan add the soy sauce, mirin, and sugar and mix. Bring to a boil and cook, stirring constantly, until all the liquid has been absorbed.

6. To cook the scrambled eggs: Beat the eggs together in a bowl. Add the sugar, sake, and a little salt to taste, and combine. Pour into a saucepan and cook initially on medium heat.

7. When the egg mixture at the rim of the pan starts to change color and lose its transparency, turn the heat down low, stirring quickly and continuously. (I usually use 4 chopsticks to do this because it stops the egg from getting lumpy and makes it very light.)

8. In another pan, lightly cook the beans, then cool them under cold running water, drain, and slice diagonally into fine strips.

9. Finally, divide the rice into individual bowls and put a little of the ground chicken, the scrambled eggs, and the beans on top, being careful not to mix them together, and serve.

In this dish the rice is cooked in a mixture of dashi stock, mirin, and soy sauce, to give it an extra level of flavor. If you want to cook more rice, simply increase the amount of liquid so it is the same as that of the rice. This way, you will be able to prepare perfect rice every time.

Rice with Soy-flavored Pork and Carrots

SERVES 4

11 oz uncooked Japanese sushi rice
1 tablespoon mirin
1 tablespoon soy sauce
1½ cups dashi stock (see page 19)
salt—to season

FOR THE PORK:

medium-sized carrot (about 5 oz)
8 oz thinly sliced pork shoulder
¼ cup soy sauce
2 tablespoons mirin
2 teaspoons sugar
pepper—to season

1. Wash the rice thoroughly, drain it, and then let it stand for 10–15 minutes.
2. Combine the mirin and soy sauce in a large liquid measuringcup. Add the dashi stock until there is 1⅔ cups of liquid. Season with salt according to taste.
3. Put the rice in a heavy saucepan and add the dashi stock mix. Cover with a tight-fitting lid and bring to a boil, then turn the heat down low and cook for 10–12 minutes. Turn off the heat and let the rice stand for a further 10 minutes, leaving the lid on.
4. To cook the pork: While the rice is cooking, peel the carrot and cut into strips ¾–1 inch long.
5. Cover the pork in plastic wrap and tenderize by hitting with a rolling pin. Then slice into ½ inch wide pieces.
6. Combine the soy sauce, mirin, and sugar in a pan and heat. Add the pork, being careful to keep the slices from sticking together. Add the carrots and cook until the liquid has almost evaporated.
7. When the rice is ready, mix together with the cooked pork and carrots, season with pepper, and serve.

Rice balls are popularly called onigiri in Japan and we love them! Where people in other countries may eat sandwiches for lunch or as a snack, we eat onigiri. I think they are so popular because they are portable and come in so many varieties. You can make them in any shape you like and use almost anything as a filling. They can be wrapped in nori seaweed to give them extra flavor and to help keep your fingers from becoming too sticky. These onigiri rice balls can be used for parties, as a snack, or in bento boxes. I like to make this recipe if I have any leftover chicken from the Three Toppings Rice recipe (see page 89).

Onigiri Rice Balls with Ground Chicken

SERVES 4

11 oz uncooked Japanese sushi rice

FOR THE GROUND CHICKEN:

7 oz boneless chicken thighs with
   skin on, ground
3 tablespoons soy sauce
1 tablespoon sake
2 tablespoons mirin
1–1½ tablespoons superfine sugar

1. Wash the rice in cold water and leave in a strainer for 10–15 minutes before cooking.
2. Put the rice in a saucepan with 1⅗ cups water, cover, and bring to a boil before reducing the heat to low and cooking for 10–12 minutes.
3. Turn off the heat and leave without taking off the lid for a further 10 minutes.
4. To cook the ground chicken: Put the chicken into a saucepan, add the soy sauce, sake, mirin, and sugar and mix together. Over medium heat, bring to a boil and cook, stirring constantly, until almost all the liquid has been absorbed. Allow to cool.
5. Mix the rice and the ground chicken together and shape into small onigiri rice balls by hand.

If I want to give rice extra flavor I often cook it with dashi stock but for this recipe I have replaced the dashi stock with a more subtle mix of water, sake, and a little salt to allow the delicate flavor of the green peas to come through. This is a versatile dish that adds color and extra taste to any meal. It is not surprising that it is one of my husband's favorite rice dishes. He particularly enjoys it served with ginger pork and a potato salad.

Green Pea Rice

SERVES 4

11 oz uncooked Japanese sushi rice

1 tablespoon sake

1 teaspoon salt

1½ cups cooked green peas

1. Wash the rice thoroughly in cold water, drain, and leave in a strainer for 10–15 minutes.
2. Put the washed rice into a heavy saucepan, add 1⅓ cups water, the sake, and salt.
3. Cover with a lid and place over high heat until it comes to a boil, then turn the heat down low and continue cooking for 10–12 minutes. Then turn the heat off and leave for a further 10 minutes, without taking the lid off.
4. When the rice is cooked, add the drained cooked peas and mix in roughly, season with a little more salt if necessary, and serve.

Rice is a wonderfully versatile ingredient. Although I love plain white rice I also often enjoy it seasoned with other ingredients, giving a variety of different flavors. This recipe, with the addition of ginger, is a good one to help you relax and I strongly recommend it to anyone who has lost their appetite or who is feeling tired—it is very reviving.

Rice with Fresh Ginger

SERVES 4

11 oz uncooked Japanese sushi rice
1¼ oz fresh ginger, peeled
3 oz shimeji mushrooms
1½ cups dashi stock (see page 19)
1 tablespoon light soy sauce
1 tablespoon mirin
1 teaspoon sake
salt—to season
nori seaweed—to serve

1. Wash the rice in cold water until the water runs clear. Drain it in a strainer, and let it stand for 10–15 minutes.
2. Chop the ginger into small pieces.
3. Trim the shimeji mushrooms and roughly chop.
4. In a large liquid measuring cup, add the dashi stock to the light soy sauce, mirin, and sake until it makes 1⅔ cups of liquid.
5. Put the rice in a heavy saucepan, and add the ginger pieces, the shimeji mushrooms, and the dashi mix.
6. Put a tight-fitting lid on the saucepan and place over high heat. When the liquid comes to a boil, turn the heat down low. After cooking for 10–12 minutes, turn off the heat and leave for a further 10 minutes, keeping the lid on.
7. Stir the rice, add a pinch of salt if desired, and serve garnished with some nori seaweed.

Mazezushi, or mixed sushi, is a type of sushi that I often make at home, particularly for parties. I have tried to make this recipe really flexible, one that can be prepared anywhere in the world with ingredients that are easy to find. There are two stages to this recipe, firstly making the rice and then mixing in a dressing and the other ingredients. On top of this mazezushi there is a mountain of golden threads made from strips of very thin egg crêpes called kinshi tamago. Once you have mastered making kinshi tamago you will be able to use it with many other recipes. It always makes any dish look spectacular.

Mazesushi

SERVES 4

11 oz uncooked Japanese sushi rice

FOR THE SUSHI DRESSING:
½ cup rice vinegar, unseasoned
2 tablespoons superfine sugar
1–1½ teaspoons salt

FOR THE MAZEZUSHI:
small carrot (about 3½ oz), peeled
1 cup mushrooms, finely sliced
3 tablespoons dashi stock
    (see page 19)
1 tablespoon soy sauce
½ tablespoon superfine sugar
½ tablespoon mirin
12 large peeled raw shrimp
1 tablespoon sake
juice of ½–1 lemon
nori seaweed—to garnish

FOR THE KINSHI TAMAGO
    CRÊPES:
4 medium eggs
1½ tablespoons superfine sugar
2 teaspoons sake
salt—to season
sunflower or vegetable oil

1. Rinse the rice thoroughly in cold water, drain, and set aside for 10–15 minutes.
2. To make the sushi dressing: Put the rice vinegar in a small saucepan and heat. When warm, add the sugar and salt. Bring to a boil and then remove from the heat and allow to cool.
3. Chop the carrot into fine julienne strips 1½ inches long.
4. Put the dashi stock, soy sauce, sugar, and mirin into a pan and heat. When it comes to a boil, add the julienned carrot and mushrooms and simmer until the carrot is just cooked. Drain.
5. Devein the shrimp and put into a saucepan with a little boiling water mixed with the sake. Simmer for 1 minute then put a lid on and leave to cool. They will cook gently in the heat of the liquid. Set aside to add later.
6. Put the washed rice in a heavy saucepan and add 1⅔ cups water. Put a lid on the pan, bring to a boil, then turn the heat down low and simmer for 10–12 minutes before turning the heat off. Leave for a further 10 minutes without removing the lid.
7. Pour the sushi dressing over the cooked rice and carefully mix in. Add the carrot and mushrooms. When cooled, add the drained shrimp, lemon juice and mix again.
8. To make the kinshi tamago crêpes: In a bowl, lightly beat the eggs together, add the sugar, sake, and season with salt. Strain the batter to ensure an evenly colored crêpe. Heat a little oil in a skillet and pour just enough egg mix to thinly coat the bottom. The crêpe will cook very quickly, so be careful to prevent it from burning. Once cooked, set the crêpe aside and repeat until all the mixture has been used. Roughly 8–10 crêpes can be made in a 7 inch skillet.
9. Slice the cooked crêpes into thin strips then loosen the pile with your fingers—you will be amazed at how their volume increases.
10. Put the rice mixture on a large serving plate, sprinkle with nori seaweed and decorate with the kinshi tamago crêpe strips on top.

Fried rice can be enjoyed all year round, I even cook it outdoors when we have a barbecue with friends and family. I like to add soy sauce flavored with garlic and ginger because I think it works well with the crabmeat and as I usually have some of the sauce ready-made in the fridge. If you have the time to make the sauce 2 weeks in advance it makes this recipe quicker and easier and also improves its flavor. The real trick of making good fried rice is to remember to keep tossing the ingredients in the wok to make sure that everything is well mixed and that the end result is light and free from lumps.

Fried Rice with Crabmeat

SERVES 2–4

5 oz cooked white crabmeat,
    without shell
¼ onion, peeled
2 scallions
3 medium eggs
salt and pepper—to season
4 tablespoons sunflower or
    vegetable oil—for frying
3½ oz ground beef
2²/₃ cups cooked Japanese sushi rice

FOR THE GARLIC AND GINGER
    SOY SAUCE:
6–9 fat cloves garlic
1½ oz fresh ginger
1²/₃ cups soy sauce

1. To make the garlic and ginger soy sauce: Slice the garlic and the ginger, add them to the soy sauce, put in a clean jar with a tight-fitting lid, and refrigerate.
2. Loosen the crabmeat flakes, making sure there are no large chunks.
3. Finely chop the onion and scallions.
4. Lightly beat the eggs in a bowl and season with salt and pepper.
5. Put a wok over high heat and add 2 tablespoons of oil. Pour in the egg mixture and fry quickly, stirring gently as it is cooking. When lightly cooked, put into a bowl and set aside.
6. Put a little more oil in the wok, add the beef, and cook, adding the onion (though not the scallion), once the beef has browned.
7. Add the rice and toss the ingredients together in the wok, adding a little more oil if necessary, until all the oil is used. Pour 3 tablespoons of the garlic and ginger soy sauce around the rim of the pan and toss all the ingredients together, ensuring that the sauce is evenly mixed in and that the rice doesn't stick.
8. Continue to toss for around 7–8 minutes, then add the crabmeat and cooked eggs, season to taste with salt and pepper, and toss the ingredients again for a further couple of minutes to heat the crabmeat through. Turn the heat off and add the scallion. Mix in thoroughly and serve piping hot.

This lovely noodle soup is a meal in itself. Noodles are very popular in Japan and are eaten noisily, especially by men who will slurp loudly. It is a sign of enjoyment and appreciation rather than bad manners, but if you are not used to it, it is hard to imitate! This recipe can also be served without the noodles if preferred – it becomes less of a main meal and more of a delicious soup that can serve up to four people.

Hot Noodle Soup with Sliced Duck

SERVES 2

7 oz duck breast with skin on
4 large scallions (about 4 oz)
2½ cups dashi stock (see page 19)
⅓ cup soy sauce
⅓ cup mirin
7 oz dried soba noodles
shichimi togarashi or chili pepper—
**   to garnish**

1. Cut the duck breasts into easy to eat slices and chop the scallions into pieces 3–3½ inches long.
2. Heat the dashi stock and then add the soy sauce and mirin. When it comes to a boil, add the duck slices. Bring back to a boil, skim the surface of any scum, add the scallions and cook for 1–2 minutes.
3. Bring a large saucepan of water to a boil. Add the soba noodles, loosening the noodles as you put them in the boiling water. When it returns to a boil, add 1 cup of cold water and continue cooking according to the instructions on the package. They should be cooked but still firm.
4. Drain the noodles and divide into two large serving bowls.
5. Pour the hot dashi soup onto the noodles and divide the pieces of duck and scallions between the two bowls. Sprinkle with shichimi togarashi and serve.

We take noodles very seriously in Japan and have many recipes that vary according to the type of noodle used. This is a very standard soba recipe that is healthy and easy to prepare. Because the soba noodles are the star of the recipe, make sure they are not overcooked and that the cooking process is stopped by draining them under cold running water. Also, enjoy the flavor of the daikon. It is a very popular vegetable in Japan and is used both raw as well as cooked. These days, it is much easier to find this useful ingredient in supermarkets around the world.

Cold Soba Noodles with Grated Daikon

SERVES 4

13 oz dried soba noodles
13 oz daikon (mooli or Japanese white radish)
1²/₃ cups mentsuyu (see below)
nori seaweed, finely sliced scallions, or leeks, washed and drained, wasabi—to garnish

FOR THE MENTSUYU:
2 x 4 inch pieces kombu seaweed (dried kelp)
1¼ cups soy sauce
1 cup mirin
scant ¼ cup superfine sugar
2 oz katsuobushi (dried fish flakes)

1. To make mentsuyu: To remove any excess saltiness from the kombu either lightly wash the kombu seaweed under running water then pat dry or wipe with a damp cloth. Put 3½ cups water in a saucepan, add the kombu, and leave for 30 minutes to 1 hour, depending on the thickness of the kombu.
2. Add the soy sauce, mirin, and sugar to the water and kombu, and place over medium heat.
3. Just before it comes to a boil add the katsuobushi and boil for 2–3 minutes, after which remove from the heat and let it stand until all the flakes have sunk to the bottom of the saucepan. Then strain into a bottle or a jar, allow to cool and then refrigerate.
4. Peel and finely grate the daikon so it looks like mashed potatoes.
5. Bring a large saucepan of water to a boil and add the soba noodles, being careful they do not stick together in the water. When it comes back to a boil, add a cup of cold water—this will help ensure the soba noodles are cooked perfectly.
6. Bring back to a boil and cook according to the package instructions.
7. When cooked, strain and rinse under running cold water, to stop the noodles from becoming too soft. Drain thoroughly.
8. Divide the noodles into individual serving bowls, place some grated daikon on top, and add the mentsuyu by carefully pouring it in at the edge of each bowl.
9. Garnish with nori seaweed, sliced scallions, and wasabi.

I often use ground meat in cooking and adding some miso paste makes the meat tastier and healthier. I use this ground meat and miso sauce with many types of noodles or rice. It makes for a very quick but impressive lunch, especially when garnished with lots of shredded cucumber and leeks on top.

Udon Noodles with a Ground Meat Miso Sauce

SERVES 4

small leek (about 2½ oz)
½ oz fresh ginger, peeled
sunflower or vegetable oil—
    for frying
13 oz ground turkey
½ cup dashi stock (see page 19)
1 tablespoon sake
2 tablespoons soy sauce
2 tablespoons mirin
1–1½ tablespoons superfine sugar
4 tablespoons awase miso (see page 21)
1 leek—to garnish
small cucumber (about 7 oz)—
    to garnish
13 oz dried udon noodles

1. Finely chop the leek and ginger. Add a little oil to a skillet and heat. Then fry the leeks and ginger until they release an aroma. Add the ground turkey and brown.

2. Mix the dashi stock, sake, soy sauce, mirin, sugar, and miso paste together and add to the ground turkey, gently cooking until it thickens.

3. Chop the leek for the garnish into fine 2 inch-long julienne and leave to soak in water for a few minutes, then drain thoroughly and set aside.

4. Cut the cucumber in half lengthwise, remove the seeds and cut first into 2 inch-wide pieces, then into fine strips.

5. Cook the udon noodles in a large saucepan of hot water, according to the instructions on the package. When cooked, drain and rinse under cold water to remove any stickiness. Drain thoroughly.

6. Place the noodles either on one large serving plate or on individual plates, and pour the sauce on top. Garnish with the julienned leeks and cucumber.

I use a wide range of noodles that can be served both hot and cold. In my house we eat fried noodles throughout the year; they make a simple, quick, and delicious meal. This particular recipe uses a very tasty mix of chicken stock, oyster sauce, and Japanese tonkatsu sauce, which can be prepared in advance and used for most fried noodle dishes, whether based on vegetables or meat. Be careful not to add the sauce too early because it will make the crispy fried noodles turn soggy. I find that the best results are achieved by not cooking too much at a time. If your skillet or wok is not very large, it may be easier to divide the ingredients and cook in batches.

Fried Noodles with Pork and Cabbage
Yaki Soba

SERVES 4

5½ oz pork shoulder

7 oz green cabbage

2 cups bean sprouts

4 packages cooked Chinese egg
   noodles (about 1 lb)

1 tablespoon chicken boullion cubes

1 tablespoon oyster sauce

5 tablespoons tonkatsu sauce

4 tablespoons sunflower or
   vegetable oil

salt and pepper—to season

ao nori (shredded nori seaweed)
   – to taste

beni shoga (red pickled ginger)
   – to garnish

1. Place some plastic wrap on a cutting board and spread the pork out on it. Cover the pork in another layer of plastic wrap and tenderize by hitting with a rolling pin. Take out of the plastic wrap and cut into ¾ inch-wide strips.

2. Shred the cabbage into 1 inch strips.

3. Top and tail the bean sprouts.

4. Ensure that the cooked noodles are untangled and loosened.

5. Mix together the chicken boullion, oyster sauce, and tonkatsu sauce and set aside.

6. Heat one tablespoon of oil in a wide skillet or wok and cook the pork, add the cabbage and bean sprouts in this order, frying them quickly on a high heat. While cooking add the rest of the oil as needed.

7. Add the cooked noodles and fry until hot, then add the sauce and season with salt and pepper.

8. Serve with a sprinkling of shredded nori seaweed and garnish with red pickled ginger on the side.

This is a very simple version of a classic Japanese dish. These individual steamed savory custards are popular with everyone. They have a very comforting and subtle flavor and there is always an element of a treasure hunt when eating them because the custards usually contain small pieces of meat or fish as well as vegetables. Once you have mastered the ratio of dashi stock to eggs you can try it with all sorts of ingredients. Drizzling a little ankake sauce on top makes this dish even tastier.

Steamed Savory Custards
Chawan Mushi

SERVES 4

4 medium eggs (approximately 7 oz in total weight)
2¹/₂ cups dashi stock (see page 19)
1 teaspoon light soy sauce
1¹/₂–2 tablespoons mirin
¹/₂–²/₃ teaspoon salt
¹/₂ cup sugar snap peas
small carrot, peeled

FOR THE ANKAKE SAUCE
1 cup dashi stock (see page 19)
2 teaspoons light soy sauce
2 tablespoons mirin
salt—to season
2 teaspoons potato starch or corn starch mixed with 2 teaspoons cold water

1. Break the eggs into a bowl and beat together thoroughly. Gradually add the dashi stock, stirring constantly. Then, using a fine sieve, strain the mixture into another bowl.
2. Add the light soy sauce, mirin, and salt to the eggs and dashi and mix together.
3. String the sugar snap peas and cut diagonally into thin strips.
4. Julienne the carrots into 1in lengths making sure they are all small enough to cook easily.
5. Divide the sugar snap peas and carrots into four individual serving dishes and pour over equal quantities of the egg mixture.
6. Bring some water in a steamer to a boil. When it is filled with steam, cover each dish with plastic wrap and place in the steamer. Steam for about 20 minutes over low heat.
7. To make the ankake sauce: Put the dashi in a saucepan, add the light soy sauce and mirin, and season with salt. Bring the dashi mix to a boil and add the potato starch and water mixture, to thicken.
8. When the custards are cooked, remove from the steamer, take off the plastic wrap, pour some ankake sauce on top of each one, and serve.

This is another classic Japanese recipe that is popular with everyone. It is one of the first recipes that students learn in their home economics classes because it is simple and requires few ingredients. I think the key to its success is how easily it can be prepared and, of course, the wonderful swirling, golden yellow color of the egg is very attractive. It looks good and tastes fantastic—a great combination.

Egg Drop Soup

SERVES 4

3 medium eggs

3½ cups dashi stock (see page 19)

1 tablespoon regular or light
    soy sauce

1 tablespoon mirin

½ teaspoon salt

1 teaspoon potato starch or
    corn starch

1. Beat the eggs in a bowl.
2. Warm the dashi stock in a saucepan. Add the light soy sauce, mirin, and salt.
3. Mix the potato starch in 2 teaspoons of cold water and set aside.
4. When the dashi comes to a boil, stir in the potato flour and water mixture—it will lightly thicken the soup.
5. Stir in the eggs and then remove from the heat to ensure the eggs are not overcooked and serve.

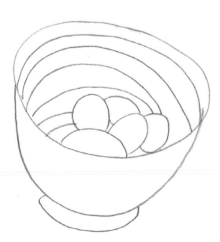

Tofu and sesame are ingredients that really complement each other and once made, this simple sesame dressing can be used with a variety of dishes. You can buy prepared sesame sauce in most Japanese supermarkets but it is easy and rewarding to make yourself. Be careful when preparing the tofu. If it is drained too much it will lose its soft texture but too little and it will be watery. Don't assemble this salad until just before you are ready to serve.

Tofu Salad with a Sesame Dressing

SERVES 4

10 oz soft/silken tofu
3½ oz bag mixed salad leaves

FOR THE SESAME SAUCE:
1 cup toasted sesame seeds
½ cup soy sauce
scant ⅓ cup superfine sugar

FOR THE SESAME DRESSING:
4 tablespoons sesame sauce
(see above)
1–2 tablespoons rice vinegar,
unseasoned
1–2 tablespoons finely chopped
leeks, washed and dried
2 teaspoons finely chopped
fresh ginger

1. To make the sesame sauce: Grind ⅔ cup of the toasted sesame seed in a mortar until sticky. Then add the soy sauce and sugar and combine. Finish by lightly grounding the remaining ⅛ cup of toasted sesame seeds. Add them to the first mixture and mix into a smooth paste.
2. Drain the tofu. Cut it in half horizontally then into four, making eight pieces in total.
3. Put the salad leaves into a bowl of iced water to crisp. Drain, dry, and refrigerate.
4. To make the sesame sauce dressing: Put the sesame sauce in a bowl, add the rice vinegar, and mix. Then add the finely chopped leeks and ginger.
5. Place the tofu on a plate, pour over the sesame dressing, put the salad leaves on top, and serve.

Over the centuries in Japanese cuisine we have taken dishes from around the world and adapted them to make them Japanese. Mabo dofu is a greatly loved dish in Japan, but was originally Chinese. My version of this recipe, using dashi stock, is lighter and milder than the original Chinese version. It is a lovely blend of spices and textures and is best served with white rice.

Tofu with a Spicy Minced Meat Sauce
Mabo Dofu

SERVES 4

1¼ cups dashi stock (see page 19)

¼ cup soy sauce

1 tablespoon superfine sugar

1 tablespoon sake

2 tablespoons mirin

2 fat cloves garlic

½ oz fresh ginger, peeled

2 scallions

1 lb 5 oz soft/silken tofu

salt

sunflower or vegetable oil—
    for frying

7 oz ground meat (usually a mix of
    pork and beef)

1–2 red chilies, seeds removed and
    finely sliced into rings

½–1 tablespoon potato starch or
    corn starch mixed with
    ½–1 tablespoon cold water

1. Combine the dashi, soy sauce, sugar, sake, and mirin in a bowl. Stir until the sugar dissolves.
2. Finely chop the garlic and ginger. Finely slice the scallions.
3. Drain then cut the tofu into ½ inch-square pieces and blanch in hot water with a little salt to firm the tofu. Drain in a strainer.
4. Heat a little oil in a deep skillet or wok and fry the garlic, ginger, and scallions.
5. Add the ground meat and brown. Add the chili and cook for a couple of minutes. Pour in the dashi mixture, bring to a boil, and then carefully add the tofu pieces.
6. Finally, thicken with the potato starch and water mixture and serve immediately.

You may be surprised that in Japan it is quite usual to prepare tofu in the same way as steak. Cooked with a great combination of garlic and leeks, and dressed with banno soy sauce, this easy to create dish has the most amazing aroma. Be careful to make sure the tofu is well drained so it fries easily. The dish is topped with a handful of the thinly shaved fish flakes, katsuobushi, which curl with the heat of the tofu and add a wonderful smoky dimension to the flavor.

Tofu Steak

SERVES 4

1 lb 5 oz soft/silken tofu

salt and pepper

2 tablespoons grated or finely
    minced garlic

1 oz fresh ginger—to garnish

3 scallions—to garnish

4–5 tablespoons potato starch or all-
    purpose flour—for coating

3–4 tablespoons sunflower or
    vegetable oil—for frying

katsuobushi (dried fish flakes)—
    to garnish

banno soy sauce—to serve

FOR THE BANNO SOY SAUCE:

½ cup mirin

1¼ cups soy sauce

4 inch piece kombu seaweed (dried
    kelp), wiped of any salty deposits

1. To make the banno soy sauce: In a small saucepan, bring the mirin to a boil, then reduce the heat to low and cook for a further 2–3 minutes to burn off the alcohol. Remove from the heat and add the soy sauce and kombu. Leave to cool then refrigerate.

2. Drain the tofu and cut into four pieces. Wipe off any excess water with paper towel.

3. Season the tofu on both sides with salt and pepper and then spread with the grated or finely minced garlic.

4. Peel and grate the ginger. Finely slice the scallions.

5. Lightly coat the tofu pieces in the potato starch.

6. Heat a little oil in a skillet and when hot add the tofu, cooking until it is crispy and browned.

7. Serve with the grated ginger, sliced scallions, and katsuobushi on top. Finish by dressing with banno soy sauce.

When friends or guests turn up unexpectedly, I will often prepare this dish. I look in my refrigerator and then use whatever I can find that works with tofu. All of these toppings are finely chopped and then used to dress a couple of blocks of smooth, creamy tofu to create a wonderful contrast of textures. It is always a good idea to put the drained tofu in the fridge on the dish that you will serve it and to put some paper towel loosely around the sides of the tofu to absorb any excess liquid.

Tofu with Crunchy Toppings

SERVES 4

1 lb 5 oz soft/silken tofu

3 slices bacon cooked until crisp

¼ cup walnuts

¼ cup scallions

¾ oz fresh ginger, minced

5 shiso leaves or a mixture of fresh
   basil and mint, shredded

garlic flakes—to taste

1 tablespoon toasted sesame seeds

FOR THE BANNO SOY SAUCE:

½ cup mirin

1¼ cups soy sauce

4 inch piece kombu seaweed (dried
   kelp), wiped of any salty deposits

1. To make the banno soy sauce: In a small saucepan, bring the mirin to a boil, then reduce the heat to low and cook for a further 2–3 minutes to burn off the alcohol. Remove from the heat and add the soy sauce and kombu. Leave to cool, then refrigerate.

2. Drain the tofu and place on a serving plate with some paper towel loosely placed around it to absorb any excess liquid. Put in the refrigerator until ready to serve.

3. Prepare the toppings by finely chopping the crispy bacon, walnuts, and scallion and mixing with the minced ginger.

4. When ready to serve, take the tofu from the refrigerator and remove the paper towel.

5. Sprinkle the toppings on the tofu and then add the shredded shiso leaves, the garlic flakes, and the sesame seeds.

6. Pour the banno soy sauce carefully around the sides of the tofu, trying not to put too much on top because it could disturb the crunchy topping arrangement and serve.

Cooking fish in miso is very traditional and is particularly popular with Japanese men. This recipe is simple with a beautiful rich flavor that is further enhanced by the addition of the ginger. I think it works particularly well with mackerel. The fish should be added to the sauce only after it has come to a boil. If you add it earlier the chances are that the fish will give off a strong odor. I like to use the sauce from cooking the fish and pour it over both the fish and the accompanying vegetables, in this case, watercress. Although this recipe is so typically Japanese, it also tastes good served with some garlic toast and a glass of white wine.

Mackerel Cooked in Miso

SERVES 2–4

8 oz fresh mackerel fillets, with skin on

1¼ oz fresh ginger

1 cup sake

3 tablespoons awase miso (see page 21)

3 tablespoons superfine sugar

¼ cup mirin

¼ cup soy sauce

heaping cup watercress—to garnish

1. Cut the mackerel in 4–5 pieces.
2. Peel the ginger and slice it thinly.
3. Put the sake, miso, sugar, mirin, and soy sauce into a saucepan and bring to a boil.
4. Place the mackerel pieces in a single layer in the liquid and add the ginger.
5. When the sauce comes to a boil again, put a lid on and cook on low heat for about 10 minutes, by which time the sauce will have reduced and thickened.
6. Serve on a plate garnished with watercress and pour the remaining sauce over the fish and watercress.

My mother taught me how to make this fantastic soup. She showed me how to grind the toasted sesame seeds into a wonderful paste, and advised me to break the tofu into pieces by hand instead of cutting with a knife, saying that this added to the enjoyment and flavor of the soup. Not only is the soup a beautiful color but it is also very healthy and has a lovely aroma. It is a good soup to have at any time of the day, even at breakfast. If I can find a sansho leaf in springtime, I like to use it as a garnish—put it on top just before serving, to give it a real taste of spring.

Miso Soup with Sesame and Tofu

SERVES 4

²/₃ cup toasted sesame seeds, plus
　　extra to garnish
3½ cups dashi stock (see page 19)
10 oz soft/silken tofu, drained
4–5 tablespoons awase miso
　　(see page 21)
sansho leaf or finely sliced
　　scallions—to garnish

1. Grind the toasted sesame seeds in a mortar with a pestle until they become sticky, almost like a paste.
2. Heat the dashi stock in a saucepan. Before it comes to a boil, add the drained tofu, tearing it into pieces before adding.
3. Gradually add the miso, stirring until completely dissolved.
4. Add the sesame paste to the soup and stir in well.
5. Bring almost to a boil then remove from the heat. Serve sprinkled with some ground sesame seeds and, if available, a sansho leaf or some finely sliced scallions.

This soup, simply known as tonjiru, is a standard dish in Japan, with each household having its own special recipe. The traditional version of the dish, made with tofu, miso, and dashi stock, combines pork with a multitude of typical Japanese vegetables like daikon, burdock, sweet potato, and konnyaku, but you can substitute these with vegetables that you have at home and it will still be delicious.

Pork and Vegetable Miso Soup
Tonjiru

SERVES 4

7 oz daikon (mooli or Japanese white radish)

small carrot (about 3½ oz)

medium-sized potato (about 5 oz)

7 oz konnyaku

7 oz thinly sliced pork

½ tablespoon sunflower or vegetable oil

1 quart dashi stock (see page 19)

2 tablespoons sake

4–5 tablespoons awase miso (see page 21)

½ leek finely sliced, washed, and drained, shichimi togarashi (or chilli pepper) —to garnish

1. Peel the daikon and carrot. Cut them lengthwise then into quarters and then slice them into ¼ inch-thick, making quarter-shaped pieces. Peel the potato and cut into bite-sized pieces. Soak in water for a few minutes to remove any excess starch, then drain. Tear the konnyaku into smaller pieces and blanch in boiling water, to remove any bitterness, then drain.

2. Cover the pork loosely in plastic wrap and, on a cutting board, tenderize by hitting with a rolling pin. Remove the cling film and cut into 1–1½ inch pieces.

3. Heat the oil in a large saucepan, add the pork and brown evenly. Add the chopped daikon, carrot, potato, and konnyaku, then the dashi stock and sake, and simmer.

4. Skim the surface when it comes to a boil. Reduce the heat and cook until the potatoes are soft.

5. Gradually add in the miso paste, stir well, and serve with the finely sliced leek and shichimi togarashi sprinkled on top.

Like most Japanese, I like to start my day with a lovely hot bowl of miso soup—it is an essential part of a Japanese breakfast. Miso is a really healthy and convenient ingredient. It is possible to make miso soup using almost any vegetables and I frequently use leftover vegetables in our family's breakfast miso soup. Try it with any of your favorite ingredients—spinach, carrots, daikon, seaweed, tofu. It works well with almost anything.

Miso Soup with Potato and Onion

SERVES 4

medium-sized potato (about 5 oz)
small onion (about 4 oz), peeled
½ cups dashi stock (see page 19)
4–5 tablespoons awase miso
    (see page 21)

1. Peel the potato, quarter it, and cut into ¼ inch-thick slices. Soak in cold water for 2–3 minutes to remove any excess starch and then drain well. Slice the onion thinly.
2. Heat the dashi in a saucepan, add the potato, and simmer.
3. When the potato is almost cooked, add the sliced onion and continue to gently simmer until the onion has softened.
4. Gradually add the miso paste, mixing it with the hot dashi in a ladle before adding directly to the soup. To achieve the best miso flavor, do not bring the soup back to the boil, serve immediately.

I nearly always add miso to any white sauce. It gives an extra depth and a softer, more rounded texture, as well as a very Japanese flavor. This white miso sauce can be used in other recipes with ingredients such as tofu and although this gratin is made with halibut, you can substitute it with most types of fish.

Halibut and Eggplant Miso Gratin

SERVES 4

FOR THE WHITE MISO SAUCE

3 tablespoons lightly salted butter

½ cup all-purpose flour

1¼ cups low-fat milk

1¼ cups heavy cream

4–5 tablespoons awase miso
(see page 21)

2 tablespoons mirin

1½ tablespoons superfine sugar

10 oz halibut fillet

medium-sized eggplant (about 13 oz)

medium-sized leek (about 10 oz)

¼ cup olive oil

salt and pepper—to season

5–7 oz grated mozzarella cheese—
for topping

1. To make the white miso sauce: Melt the butter in a saucepan. Add the flour and make a roux, continuously stirring to ensure it doesn't burn. Gradually add the milk to the pan, again continuously stirring to avoid it becoming lumpy. Bring to a slow boil and add the cream, then the miso, mirin, and sugar in that order, mixing thoroughly, then set aside.

2. Cut the halibut fillet into 2½ inch pieces.

3. Make stripes in the skin of the eggplant using a potato peeler then cut into ¾ inch diagonal pieces. Soak them in water for a few minutes to reduce any bitterness, drain well, and pat dry.

4. Cut the leeks into ¾ inch diagonal pieces, then wash and drain thoroughly.

5. Heat 3 tablespoons of the olive oil in a skillet and fry the eggplant. Add the leeks and cook gently. Remove from the skillet and set aside.

6. Add the remaining olive oil to the skillet and lightly brown the fish. Season with salt and pepper.

7. Take the eggplant, leeks, and fish and add to the miso white sauce, mixing in carefully.

8. Put into an ovenproof casserole dish, top with grated mozzarella, and bake in a preheated oven for 20 minutes at 400°F.

This delicious pickled ginger is usually served with sushi but it can also be an accompaniment to many other dishes. It may look as though it is difficult to make, but in fact it is very easy: all you have to do is boil the ginger in a sweet vinegar mixture. Once made, it can be kept for two to three weeks in the refrigerator and so can be enjoyed on many occasions.

Sweet Pickled Ginger
Gari

4 oz fresh ginger, peeled and thinly
    sliced

FOR THE SWEETENED VINEGAR:
½ cup rice vinegar, unseasoned
½ tablespoon mirin
1–2 tablespoons superfine sugar
1 teaspoon salt

1. To make the sweetened vinegar: Combine all the ingredients in a bowl. Stir well until the salt and sugar are completely dissolved.
2. Slice the ginger as thinly as possible. If available, use a mandoline.
3. Put the ginger into a small saucepan of boiling water and simmer until it just changes color. Be careful not to overcook it or it will lose its lovely flavor and aroma. Drain.
4. Dry the sliced ginger then add, while still hot, to the sweetened vinegar.
5. Leave in the refrigerator for at least half a day before using to let the ginger develop a rich full flavor.

I love using both white and black sesame seeds in my recipes. They add texture, aroma, flavor, and color. I use a lot of sesame when cooking, and preparing vegetables with a sesame dressing is very common in Japan. I always prepare the dressing in advance and keep some in the refrigerator ready for use. Sesame seeds should always be toasted before use, taking care not to burn them. It gives them an extra special flavor and makes them easier to make into a paste. If you cannot find sesame seeds or paste, you can use peanut butter or tahini as a substitute. Please experiment with this dressing—try combining it with other ingredients such as rice vinegar, miso paste, or dashi stock to make new sauces and dressings.

Green Beans with a Sesame Dressing

SERVES 4

2 cups green beans

FOR THE SESAME DRESSING:
⅓ cup toasted sesame seeds
2 tablespoons superfine sugar
½ tablespoon mirin
½–1 tablespoon soy sauce
salt—to season

1. Prepare the green beans, lightly cook in a pan of boiling water with a little salt, then drain and rinse under cold running water and pat dry.
2. To make the sesame dressing: Put the sesame seeds into a mortar, preferably a Japanese mortar with a grooved interior. Grind the seeds until they are almost a paste then add the sugar, mirin, and soy sauce and mix well. Add a little salt if needed.
3. Mix the sesame dressing in with the green beans and serve. The paste can also be made in a food processor but be careful not to overprocess.

Pumpkin is a very popular vegetable in Japan. Although it is sweet it is often served as a side dish with the main part of a meal or as a dessert or even with tea in the afternoon. In this recipe the sweet flavor of the pumpkin is a great combination with the aroma of the sesame. Japanese pumpkins have quite thin skins so I don't usually peel them but if the available pumpkins have a thick skin, then remove it.

Pumpkin with a Sweet Sesame Glaze

SERVES 4–6

2 lb pumpkin (about 1½ lb without seeds and string)
¼–⅓ cup superfine sugar
1 tablespoon light soy sauce
scant ¼ cup ground toasted sesame seeds

1. Peel the pumpkin if necessary, then remove the seeds and pith and cut into 1 inch square pieces.
2. Put 1–1½ cups water, the sugar, and light soy sauce in a saucepan to heat. When it comes to a boil, add the pumpkin pieces.
3. Cook the pumpkin, constantly stirring once the liquid has reduced to prevent it from sticking or burning. When all the liquid has been absorbed and the pumpkin is soft and sticky, turn off the heat and leave to cool.
4. When cooled, add the ground sesame seeds, mix together, and serve.

Fresh vegetables are best eaten raw and I love serving them with a variety of dips. I think it makes a nice change to use this sesame sauce in this way. I like to use whatever I find in my refrigerator but for this book I have used cherry tomatoes, celery, carrots, and cauliflower. You can adjust the quantities to suit the number of people eating.

Vegetables with a Sesame Dip

SERVES 6

FOR THE SESAME DIP:
1 cup toasted sesame seeds
½ cup soy sauce
scant ⅓ cup superfine sugar

1⅓ cups cherry tomatoes
2 stalks celery
small carrot (about 4 oz)
8 oz cauliflower

1. To make the sesame sauce: Grind ⅔ cup of the toasted sesame seeds with a mortar and pestle until they develop a pastelike consistency. In a bowl, mix the soy sauce with the sugar, add the ground sesame seeds, and mix well. Lightly grind the remaining ⅓ cup of sesame seeds and add to make a smooth paste.
2. Wash the cherry tomatoes.
3. Remove any stringy parts of the celery and chop into 2½ inch sticks.
4. Peel the carrot and chop into 2½ inch-long, ¾ inch-wide batons.
5. Chop the cauliflower into bite-sized florets, wash, and dry.
6. Arrange the vegetables around the bowl of the sesame dip.

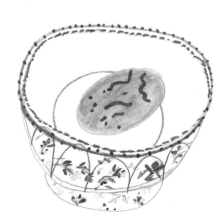

I love watercress both cooked or raw in a salad. This recipe works with watercress or with most other green vegetables like broccoli, asparagus, or spinach. Peanut butter is commonly available in most homes, so it is an easy dish to make at any time.

Watercress with a Light Peanut Dressing

SERVES 4

7 cups watercress

a little salt

**4 tablespoons peanut butter
(crunchy or smooth)**

1½ tablespoons soy sauce

1½—2 tablespoons mirin

1. Wash the watercress then cut into 1in lengths, separating the leaves from the stems.
2. Boil some water in a saucepan and when it comes to a boil, add a little salt and then the watercress, adding the stems first.
3. Cook until the stems are slightly softened, then drain and rinse under cold running water. Lightly squeeze to remove any excess water.
4. Put the peanut butter in a bowl, add the soy sauce and mirin, and combine to make a smooth dressing.
5. Add the watercress to the dressing and mix in, ensuring it is well coated. Season, if necessary, with a little salt.

Although this is a simple recipe, it is one that is very much enjoyed in all Japanese homes and is a dish I like to eat when tired. The combination of lightly cooked vegetables, katsuobushi dried fish flakes, and soy sauce makes for a tasty recipe that can be used with most vegetables. If I need a vegetable dish at short notice, this is one that I often use.

Lightly Cooked Spinach with Soy Sauce

SERVES 4

7 cups spinach (about 7oz)
banno soy sauce or regular soy sauce
katsuobushi (dried fish flakes)—to garnish

FOR THE BANNO SOY SAUCE:
½ cup mirin
1¼ cups soy sauce
4 inch piece kombu seaweed (dried kelp), wiped of any salty deposits

1. To make the banno soy sauce: In a small saucepan, bring the mirin to a boil, then reduce the heat to low and cook for a further 2–3 minutes to burn of the alcohol. Take off the heat and add the soy sauce and kombu. Cool and refrigerate.
2. Wash and trim the spinach, if necessary. Separate the leaves from the stems and then chop into 2 inch pieces.
3. Bring some water to a boil in a medium-sized saucepan, add a little salt, and then add the stems and leaves of the spinach. Briefly cook, then rinse under cold running water and drain.
4. Squeeze the spinach firmly to get rid of any excess water, then loosen the leaves by hand.
5. Place on a plate or a bowl, garnish with some katsuobushi, and dress with some of the banno soy sauce or regular soy sauce.

I was so surprised when I first saw the size of cucumbers outside Japan—they are enormous and very watery inside. In Japan, cucumbers are small and crispy. If you cannot find a Japanese cucumber, scoop out the seeds from inside before making this recipe. This dish is good to serve with most meals.

Quick Pickled Cucumber

SERVES 4

½ cup soy sauce

½ cup rice vinegar, unseasoned

4 tablespoons sugar

sesame oil—to taste

large cucumber (about 1–1¼ lb)

2 teaspoons salt

1¼ oz fresh ginger, peeled

1. Mix together the soy sauce, rice vinegar, sugar, and sesame oil and set aside.
2. Trim the ends of the cucumber. Rub the cucumber with the salt for a few minutes and then wash the salt off. This will help remove any bitterness from the skin and give it a nice color.
3. Cut the cucumber in half lengthwise and remove the seeds with a spoon. Hit gently with a rolling pin to roughly break it up, and then chop into bite-sized pieces.
4. Finely chop the ginger into julienne.
5. Put the cucumber and ginger into a plastic food bag and add the liquid mixture prepared in step 1. Refrigerate for at least 2–3 hours before serving. The pickled cucumber can be kept for a couple of days before it will lose its crunchy texture.

My hometown of Shimoda is a seaside town located at the bottom of the Izu Peninsula. I grew up eating a fantastic diet of seafood, and not only fish but also seaweed. We use many types of seaweed in Japanese food. The best known are nori, a crispy dried seaweed often used in sushi; kombu, a large dried kelp mainly used to flavor stocks like dashi; hijiki, used when reconstituted in salads, and wakame, used in this recipe. The wakame in this light vinegar dressing is one of my favorite flavors from my childhood.

Cucumber and Wakame Seaweed in a Sweet Pickled Dressing

SERVES 4

¼ oz dried wakame seaweed
medium-sized cucumber (about 13 oz)
salt
²/₃ cup rice vinegar, unseasoned
2 tablespoons superfine sugar
grated fresh ginger—to taste

1. Wash and then soak the wakame seaweed for around 10 minutes, then cut into bite-sized pieces and set aside.
2. Cut the cucumber in half lengthwise and scoop out the seeds with a spoon, then slice diagonally into pieces ¼ inch thick.
3. Place in a bowl, lightly sprinkle some salt over the slices, and leave for 5–10 minutes. Then squeeze firmly and place in a clean bowl.
4. Combine a pinch of salt, vinegar, and sugar in a bowl and mix well, then add the cucumber and wakame seaweed and leave in the refrigerator to chill before serving. Please be careful not to refrigerate for too long because the wakame and cucumber will lose their color and texture.
5. Serve in small dishes with a pat of grated ginger on top.

In Japan, asparagus stems tend to be quite big, so I was really surprised to see how small asparagus is outside of Japan. A shiraae is a very versatile Japanese dish that can be made with most types of vegetable and always has a tofu-based dressing. I like to adjust the amounts of sesame paste and miso to create the best blend for any particular vegetable, making a creamy dressing by adding ripe avocado or changing the texture by adding it diced. This particular recipe works well with young asparagus.

Asparagus Shiraae

SERVES 4

10 oz soft/silken tofu

1 bunch (7 oz) green asparagus

4 tablespoons ground toasted
    sesame seeds

2 tablespoons superfine sugar

1 teaspoon light soy sauce

½ teaspoon awase miso (see page 21)

salt—to season

1. Drain the tofu and remove any excess water by wrapping it in paper towel and weighing it down with something like a plate.
2. Remove the woody part of the asparagus and then cut each spear diagonally into three.
3. Bring some water to the boil, add a little salt and lightly cook the asparagus for a few minutes. The asparagus should still be firm when drained. Cool under cold running water and pat dry.
4. Put the tofu in a bowl and add the ground sesame seeds, sugar, light soy sauce, and miso. Combine thoroughly.
5. Add the asparagus to the bowl and mix into the dressing, seasoning with extra salt if required.
6. Serve either in one serving dish or in individual bowls.

This is one of my top three favorite recipes and it is one my family loves, too. It is important to prepare the eggplant by soaking the cut pieces for 5–10 minutes before cooking. In Japan we always start by chopping then soaking vegetables like eggplant and burdock before preparing them; by doing this you remove any bitter flavors.

Eggplant in Spicy Sauce

SERVES 4

1 lb 3 oz eggplant
⅓ cup soy sauce
⅓ cup mirin
2½ tablespoons superfine sugar
¼ cup rice vinegar, unseasoned
sunflower or vegetable oil –
    for deep-frying
2–3 tablespoons finely minced leeks
    or scallions
1 teaspoon finely minced garlic
1 teaspoon finely minced fresh ginger
1–2 red chilies, seeds removed and
    finely sliced into rings
shredded leek washed and drained—
    to garnish

1. Trim the eggplant and, using a potato peeler, make some stripes in its skin. Then cut into 1in thick disks and then quarters. Place them into a bowl of cold water, soak for 5–10 minutes, then drain and pat dry.
2. Combine the soy sauce, mirin, sugar, and rice vinegar to make a sauce and set aside.
3. In a skillet, heat enough oil to cover the eggplant. When hot, add the eggplant pieces and deep-fry at a medium-high temperature (340°F).
4. When the eggplant is cooked (when it is soft in the middle) remove from the skillet and drain off any excess oil. Put in a bowl, add the sauce, then the minced leek, garlic, ginger, and chili and combine.
5. Serve with some shredded leek on top.

This recipe came about as a result of trial and error. My friend had a surfeit of baby tomatoes so she gave them to me to see if I could use them. I made lots of dishes, salads, tomato sauces, and so on, but I still had some left over, so I decided to try to make pickled tomatoes. The first batch didn't work very well, so I pricked the tomatoes first to absorb more of the pickling vinegar. They were a great success and now I regularly serve them, often on a bed of ice for a really cool treat.

Lightly Pickled Tomatoes

4 cups cherry tomatoes

FOR THE PICKLING VINEGAR:
1¼ cups rice vinegar, unseasoned
scant ¼ cup superfine sugar
1 teaspoon salt

1. To make the pickling vinegar: Combine the vinegar, sugar, and salt in a bowl and stir until the sugar and salt have dissolved.
2. Wash the tomatoes, dry, and remove any stalks.
3. Prick each tomato a few times with a toothpick.
4. Place in a sterilized glass storage jar and then add the pickling vinegar. Keep in the refrigerator for up to 3–4 days.

Everyone loves the combination of steak with mashed potatoes. My husband particularly enjoys it, so I have often found myself preparing it. In an effort to give variety and interest, I have made a traditional ankake sauce with mushrooms to accompany the mashed potatoes. I think that this classic Western dish is made more interesting by the addition of a Japanese sauce like this because it works really well together and gives an old standard a new twist.

Mashed Potatoes with a Japanese-style Mushroom Sauce

SERVES 4

1½ cups chestnut or button
   mushrooms
3½ oz enoki mushrooms
large scallion
1 lb potatoes
²/₃ cup cream
salt—to season
1²/₃ cups dashi stock (see page 19)
2 tablespoons light soy sauce
1 tablespoon mirin
a pinch of superfine sugar
1 tablespoon potato starch or corn
   starch mixed with 1 tablespoon
   cold water

1. Trim the stems of the chestnut mushrooms and then chop into quarters. Cut off and discard the root of the enoki mushrooms then chop into ½ inch-wide pieces. Slice the scallion into ½ inch pieces.
2. Peel the potatoes and chop into bite-sized pieces. Soak in water for a couple of minutes to remove any excess starch and drain. Cook the potato pieces in boiling water until soft, then drain.
3. Mash the potatoes while hot, add the cream to make a really smooth mixture, and then season with salt.
4. Put the dashi stock into a saucepan and bring to a boil. Add the light soy sauce, mirin, and sugar. After the sugar has dissolved, add the chestnut and enoki mushrooms. Boil briefly, until the mushrooms are just softening, then reduce the heat and check the seasoning again, adding more salt if necessary.
5. Finally, thicken the mushroom sauce by stirring in the potato starch and water mixture, then add the sliced scallion. Serve the mashed potatoes with the mushroom sauce poured on top.

When I travel to London I love to go and look around the supermarkets at the different products. I am always amazed by the variety of potatoes available. I have tried many of these potatoes and thought that this typical, slightly sweet Japanese shrimp and chicken sauce, which is often served with rice, would work very well with potatoes, particularly small new potatoes. I think you will be surprised at how tasty the combination of meat and seafood is. It is worth experimenting with this sauce because it works well with other types of meat and vegetables.

New Potatoes with Shrimp and Chicken Japanese-style

SERVES 4

2 lb new potatoes

1 cup dashi stock (see page 19)

1 tablespoon soy sauce

1 tablespoon light soy sauce

1 tablespoon sake

1 tablespoon superfine sugar

2 tablespoons mirin

FOR THE SHRIMP AND CHICKEN SAUCE:

7 oz peeled raw shrimp

4 shiitake or chestnut mushrooms

small carrot (about 2oz), peeled

3½ oz ground chicken

1²/₃ cups dashi stock (see page 19)

1 tablespoon soy sauce

2 tablespoons light soy sauce

2 tablespoons sake

2 tablespoons mirin

3 tablespoons superfine sugar

a little salt

1 tablespoon potato starch or corn starch mixed with 1 tablespoon cold water

1. Wash the potatoes. If you are using slightly old potatoes, peel them and cut them into smaller pieces, similar to the size of new potatoes. Soak the potatoes for 2–3 minutes to remove any excess starch, then drain and put in a saucepan.

2. Add the dashi stock, soy sauces, sake, sugar, and mirin to the potatoes and bring to a boil. Make a drop lid out of some aluminum foil (it should fit tightly inside the pan) and rest it on top of the potatoes. Then turn the heat down low and simmer until most of the liquid has been absorbed. Remove from the heat and keep warm.

3. To make the shrimp and chicken sauce: Devein the shrimp and mince it.

4. Trim and dice the mushrooms. Dice the carrot.

5. Combine the ground chicken, mushrooms, and carrot in a bowl and mix well.

6. Put the dashi stock, soy sauces, sake, mirin, and sugar in a saucepan and bring to a boil. Add the ground chicken, mushroom, and carrot mixture, loosening the chicken as you add it. When it all comes back to a boil, skim the surface of any scum, add the ground shrimp, and season with salt.

7. The chicken and shrimp will cook fairly quickly so be careful not to overcook. Thicken by adding the potato flour and water mixture, stirring as you do so.

8. Put the potatoes on a deep plate and pour the shrimp and chicken mixture on top and serve.

Seeing so many different types of potatoes in Europe really inspired me to create new recipes using them. Here I dress the potatoes with both butter and soy sauce—a surprisingly good combination. For this dish it is better to chop the potatoes into large pieces.

Potatoes with a Sweet Soy Dressing

SERVES 4

4 medium potatoes
   (about 1¼ lb in total)
1½–2 tablespoons soy sauce
2 tablespoons superfine sugar
1 tablespoon lightly salted butter

1. Peel the potatoes, quarter each , and then soak the pieces for a couple of minutes to remove any excess starch. Boil them in a large pan of water until cooked, then drain and set aside.
2. Put the soy sauce and sugar in a pan over medium heat until the sugar has dissolved.
3. Add the boiled potatoes and stir them around until fully coated with the sauce. Turn down the heat and let them simmer for a while to absorb the flavor, gently tossing the potatoes continuously so they do not burn.
4. Finally, add the butter, stir again, and serve.

One of my favorite ingredients is carrots and I especially love the crispy carrots I have tasted in Britain. This dish is made with my light pickling vinegar, which is not as sharp or acidic as pickling vinegars used outside of Japan. This recipe is delicious as a condiment, but with its wonderful crunchy texture it can also be drained and served as an accompanying salad to Parma ham, cooked octopus, or even sashimi drizzled with olive oil and sprinkled with Parmesan cheese.

Lightly Pickled Julienne Carrots and Celery

SERVES 4

2 medium-sized carrots (about 10 oz)
3 stalks celery (about 7 oz)
3¼ oz fresh ginger

FOR THE PICKLING VINEGAR:
1 cup mirin
1 cup rice vinegar, unseasoned
2–3 tablespoons superfine sugar
2 teaspoons salt

1. To make the pickling vinegar: Heat the mirin in a small saucepan. When it comes to a boil, turn the heat down low and simmer for 3 minutes. Remove from the heat and add the rice vinegar, sugar, and salt while still hot. Stir until the sugar and salt are dissolved, then cool.

2. Peel the carrots, remove any stringy parts from the celery, and chop both the carrots and celery into julienne strips 2 inches long. Peel the ginger and cut into similar sized strips.

3. Put the carrot, celery, and ginger in a storage jar. Pour the pickling vinegar over and refrigerate. It can be kept refrigerated for up to 1 week.

I adore carrots and was surprised to find that carrots outside Japan taste different, as well as having a slightly different texture—other varieties are often harder than Japanese. After spending hours chopping them finely for a recipe, I had the idea of adding grated carrots to this salad instead.

Crispy Salad with Grated Carrots and Ponzu Soy Dressing

SERVES 4

1 package mixed salad leaves
small carrot (about 3 oz)
¼ cup ponzu soy sauce (see below)
1 tablespoon sesame oil

FOR THE PONZU SOY SAUCE:
½ cup mirin
½ cup soy sauce
¼ cup lemon juice
2 inch piece kombu seaweed (dried kelp), wiped of any salty deposits

1. To make the ponzu soy sauce: Put the mirin in a small saucepan, bring to a boil then reduce the heat to low and cook for a further 2–3 minutes to burn off the alcohol. Take off the heat and add the soy sauce, lemon juice, the piece of kombu seaweed, and stir to combine. Leave to cool, then refrigerate.
2. To make the salad leaves crispy, soak them in iced water then drain well and put in the refrigerator until ready to dress.
3. Peel and grate the carrot.
4. When you are ready to serve, mix the ponzu soy sauce and sesame oil together to make a dressing.
5. Put the salad leaves on a serving plate and sprinkle the grated carrot on top. Pour the dressing over and serve immediately.

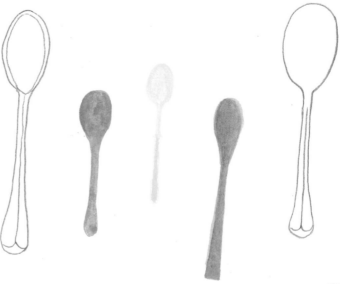

Many years ago I was invited to a foreign friend's house. I had not had much experience of traveling overseas at the time and I was really taken aback at being served raw cauliflower. It was dished up as an hors d'oeuvre with a dipping sauce and I now realize it is fairly common outside Japan, but at that time, I was really surprised. As a result of this experience, I started experimenting with raw cauliflower, slicing it into salads and other dishes. However, for this recipe lightly cooked cauliflower works best. This makes a lovely hors d'oeuvre, served with drinks or as an accompaniment to a curry.

Hot Lightly Pickled Cauliflower

1 lb cauliflower

3 tablespoons sunflower or
    vegetable oil

3 fat cloves garlic, thinly sliced

2 red chilies, seeds removed and
    roughly chopped

1 tablespoon chicken boullion cubes

½ cup rice vinegar, unseasoned

1 teaspoon soy sauce

1. Chop the cauliflower into bite-sized pieces.
2. Heat the oil in a skillet and sauté the sliced garlic. When the aroma is released, add the cauliflower and the red chilies and sauté quickly over high heat.
3. Turn off the heat. Add the rice vinegar and the chicken boullion cubes and mix in quickly. Season with soy sauce and serve.

This is a real contrast to the more commonly known coleslaw recipe using mayonnaise. This dish is extremely light and very simple. It can be prepared quickly and easily and is absolutely delicious. Please make sure you use toasted sesame seeds in this recipe.

Japanese Coleslaw Salad

SERVES 4

10 oz green cabbage
half a small onion, peeled
1 teaspoon sunflower
    or vegetable oil
¼ cup rice vinegar, unseasoned
1–2 teaspoons superfine sugar
light soy sauce—to taste
salt and pepper—to season
4 tablespoons toasted sesame seeds

1. Shred the cabbage and onion. Soak them in iced water for 2 or 3 minutes, drain well, and store in a container in the refrigerator for about 30 minutes. This will give the cabbage and the onion an extra crunchiness.

2. When ready to serve, remove them from the refrigerator and add the oil, rice vinegar, sugar, and light soy sauce in this order, mixing in each ingredient quickly.

3. Season with salt and pepper, sprinkle the sesame seeds on top, and serve immediately.

One day I found I only had some leeks and mushrooms in my refrigerator but I needed to make a vegetable dish for dinner. This led to the creation of this easy to prepare, tasty recipe. It is so simple but the addition of soy sauce and sake gives it extra flavor and makes it a little more special. This dish is best made with either baby leeks or scallions.

Sautéed Leeks and Mushrooms

SERVES 4

6 oz baby leeks or scallions

1½ cups shiitake mushrooms

3 tablespoons sunflower or
    vegetable oil

2 tablespoons sake

2 tablespoons soy sauce or ginger
    and garlic soy sauce

shichimi togarashi or chili pepper—
    to taste

1. Cut the leeks or scallions into 2–2½ inch long pieces and then into strips.
2. Trim the shiitake mushrooms and then slice diagonally into 1 inch pieces.
3. Heat the oil in a large skillet. Add the shiitake mushrooms and leeks and brown. When the leeks have softened, add the sake and then the soy sauce.
4. Serve with shichimi togarashi or chili pepper on top.

I am always looking for new ideas for vegetable dishes and this simple recipe is a really good way to serve a large variety of them in a tasty sauce. As I mentioned in the introduction, there are various sauces that can be used in so many situations, and one of those sauces is this mentsuyu sauce. I think the vegetables in this recipe should be chopped smaller than usual to make the dish look more attractive and easier to eat. It can be kept in the fridge for up to three to four days, can be eaten hot or cold, and can be made with almost any combination of vegetables—a very versatile recipe for any season.

Mixed Vegetables in Mentsuyu Sauce

SERVES 4–6

1 slender eggplant (about 7 oz)

7 oz winter squash flesh, without
    string or seeds

7 oz parsnips, peeled

10 okra

1 red pepper (around 3½ oz)

1 yellow pepper (around 3½ oz)

sunflower or vegetable oil—for
    deep-frying

FOR THE MENTSUYU:

1²/₃ cups dashi stock (see page 19)

⅓ cup soy sauce

2 tablespoons mirin

1 tablespoon superfine sugar

1. To make the mentsuyu: Combine the dashi, soy sauce, mirin, and sugar in a small saucepan over a high heat and bring to a boil. Then remove from the heat and allow to cool before putting in a deep serving dish and setting aside.
2. Trim the eggplant and cut in half lengthwise. Cut each half into six pieces and soak in water for 5 minutes to remove any bitterness. Then drain and pat dry.
3. Cut the squash into 1 inch pieces.
4. Cut each pepper in half lengthwise. Remove the seeds and cut into thin, bite-sized pieces.
5. Cut the parsnip into 1 inch pieces.
6. Trim the okra.
7. Take all the vegetable pieces and deep-fry them. When lightly cooked, drain on a rack or on some paper towel to remove any excess oil, and add to the mentsuyu mixture while still hot.
8. Serve hot or cold.

I love eating vegetables and am always looking for new ways to serve them. I think this combination of lightly cooked vegetables with a miso dressing is just delicious and yet it is so easy to prepare. You can use any vegetables but be careful not to overcook them—they should be crispy with a firm bite. If the miso dressing is a little thick, a little dashi stock can be added to thin it out.

Vegetable Salad with a Miso Dressing

SERVES 4

1 cup green beans
1½ cups cauliflower florets
1½ cups broccoli florets
shichimi togarashi or chili pepper—
    to taste

FOR THE DRESSING:
13 oz awase miso (see page 21)
½ cup sake
1 cup mirin
heaping ⅓ cup superfine sugar

1. To make the miso dressing: Combine all the ingredients in a saucepan over medium heat. When it comes to a boil, turn the heat down low and continue to cook for around 20 minutes, stirring regularly to ensure it does not burn. Then remove, cool, and refrigerate. It will keep in the fridge for 2–3 weeks.
2. To make the salad: Prepare the green beans and cut each on the diagonal into three pieces.
3. Boil some water in a large saucepan and add the broccoli and cauliflower florets and the green beans in this order and quickly blanch them. Do not overcook—the vegetables should remain crunchy. Rinse them under cold, running water and drain.
4. Lightly dry the vegetables and place in a bowl, dress with 3 tablespoons of the miso dressing, and sprinkle with some shichimi togarashi according to taste.

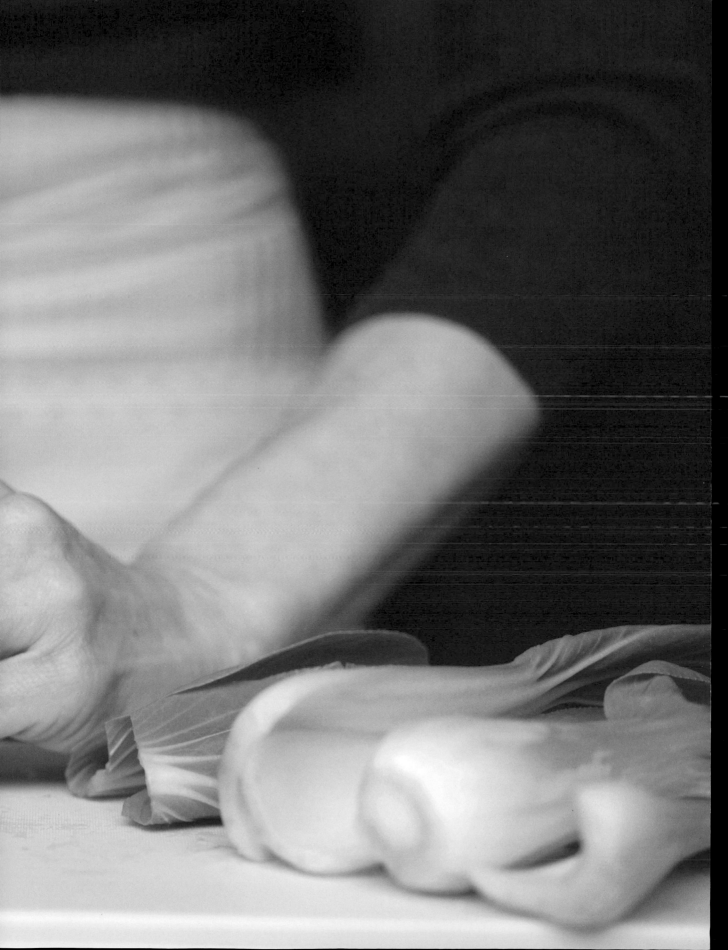

Stockists

In addition to local Japanese and Asian food markets, the Internet offers an array of sources for hard-to-find ingredients and equipment. Below are just a few suggestions.

AMAZON.COM
www.amazon.com
Asian foods and cookware

ASIA FOODS
www.asiafoods.com
Asian foods

ASIAN FOOD GROCER
www.asianfoodgrocer.com
Asian foods

ETHNIC FOODS
www.ethnicfoods.com
Asian foods

EDEN FOODS
www.edenfoods.com
Asian foods

KALUSTYAN'S
www.kalustyans.com
Asian and other specialty ingredients

KOAMART
www.koamart.com
Asian foods

KITAZAWA SEED CO.
www.kitazawaseed.com
Asian and other seeds

MITSUWA
www.mitsuwa.com
Asian foods and cookware

NET GROCER
www.netgrocer.com

PACIFIC RIM GOURMET
www.pacificrimgourmet.com
Asian foods and cookware

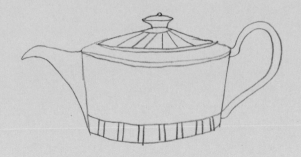

First published in 2009 by Conran Octopus Ltd
a part of Octopus Publishing Group
2–4 Heron Quays, London E14 4JP
www.octopusbooks.co.uk

An Hachette Livre UK Company
www.hachettelivre.co.uk

Distributed in the United States and Canada by Octopus Books USA,
c/o Hachette Book Group USA, 237 Park Avenue, New York, NY 10017 USA
www.octopusbooksusa.com

Text copyright © Harumi Kurihara 2009;
Design and Layout copyright © Conran Octopus 2009;
Photographs copyright © Jason Lowe 2009

British Cataloguing-in-Publication Data. A catalogue record for this
book is available from the British Library.

Publisher: Lorraine Dickey
Text: Harumi Kurihara and Sue Hudson
Project Coordination: Sue Hudson and FCI London
Managing Editor: Sybella Marlow

Art Direction and Design: Jonathan Christie
Photography: Jason Lowe
Illustrations: Kim Marsland

Production Manager: Katherine Hockley

ISBN 978 1 84091 544 0
Printed and bound in China